EVALUATING WRITING:
Describing, Measuring, Judging

EVALUATING WRITING:
Describing, Measuring, Judging

Charles R. Cooper • Lee Odell

State University of New York at Buffalo

Library of Congress Cataloging in Publication Data
Main entry under title:

Evaluating writing.

  Bibliography: p.
  1. English language—Composition and exercises—
Ability testing. 2. English language—Rhetoric—Ability
testing. I. Cooper, Charles Raymond, 1934-
II. Odell, Lee.
PE1404.E9   808'.042'076   77-11991
ISBN 0-8141-1622-1

CONTENTS

INTRODUCTION   vii

HOLISTIC EVALUATION OF WRITING   3
Charles R. Cooper
State University of New York at Buffalo

PRIMARY TRAIT SCORING   33
Richard Lloyd-Jones
University of Iowa

COMPUTER-AIDED DESCRIPTION OF MATURE   69
WORD CHOICES IN WRITING
Patrick J. Finn
State University of New York at Buffalo

EARLY BLOOMING AND LATE BLOOMING   91
SYNTACTIC STRUCTURES
Kellogg W. Hunt
Emeritus, Florida State University

MEASURING CHANGES IN INTELLECTUAL PROCESSES   107
AS ONE DIMENSION OF GROWTH IN WRITING
Lee Odell
State University of New York at Buffalo

INDIVIDUALIZED GOAL SETTING, SELF-EVALUATION,   135
AND PEER EVALUATION
Mary H. Beaven
Virginia Commonwealth University

INTRODUCTION

The purpose of this book is to provide a comprehensive summary of the best current information on describing writing and measuring growth in writing. The authors have tried to keep in mind the concerns of researchers and curriculum evaluators and of teachers in secondary schools and colleges. We hope the information we present here will help solve some of the complex and perplexing problems of evaluating the writing performance of secondary school and college students.

Early drafts of each chapter were prepared as papers for the Conference on Describing Writing and Measuring Growth in Writing held prior to the 1975 San Diego Annual Convention of the National Council of Teachers of English. The conference was planned and cochaired by the editors of this book.

At the conference and later in revising the papers, we attempted to answer these questions:

1 When we describe writing and measure students' growth in writing, what should we look at? Should we examine only the written product? Should we examine the processes or strategies which generated that product? In either case, what facets of the product, what aspects of the process should we examine when we describe/measure so complex a thing as growth in writing?

2 How can we find out how well an individual performs at a certain stage in his or her development as a writer? To ask it another way: How can we determine precisely what a writer is doing and not doing so that we can plan efficient, focused instruction?

3 How can we measure growth in writing ability over a period of time?

4 How can we involve students in the evaluation of writing?

As a result of recent developments in theory and research findings, we discovered that we could answer these questions with some confidence. We knew at the outset that we were unwilling to settle for the kinds of information provided by published standardized tests of writing because we did not believe they assessed students' ability to compose for different purposes and audiences. During our interactions at the conference, and later in revising our papers, we were relieved and pleased to be able to affirm that valid evaluations of writing performance are possible. Such evaluations are time-consuming; but for reasons we shall explain, they are greatly preferable to standardized tests that purport to measure writing ability.

The specific contributions of the authors follow:

- Charles Cooper reviews various approaches to holistic evaluation, giving particular attention to analytic scales.
- Richard Lloyd-Jones presents a promising new holistic scoring procedure, Primary Trait Scoring, which was developed for use in a nation-wide assessment of writing performance.
- Patrick Finn describes how the computer can be used to characterize maturity of word choice in students' papers and incidentally raises a number of interesting questions about word choice.
- Kellogg Hunt reviews some new and unpublished research that affirms his and Francis Christensen's earlier findings about the development of syntactic fluency in school-age writers.
- Lee Odell outlines a procedure for identifying the basic intellectual strategies writers use in formulating and presenting their ideas and feelings.
- Mary Beaven presents a careful critique of three ways to involve students in evaluating: individualized goal setting, self-evaluation, and peer evaluation.

Conspicuously absent from this list of articles is any extended discussion of standardized tests of writing. Although widely used, standardized tests measure only editorial skills—choosing the best sentence, recognizing correct usage, punctuation, and capitalization. At least for this reason, tests are not valid measures of writing performance. The only justifiable uses for standardized, norm-referenced tests of editorial skills are for prediction or placement or for the criterion measure in a research study with a narrow "correctness" hypothesis. But even their use for placement is not as valid as a single writing sample quickly scored by trained raters, as in the screening for Subject A classes (remedial writing) at the University of California campuses. In instances where a writing sample is impossible to obtain for tentative placement or exemption, we would prefer a simple verbal ability measure like the Scholastic Aptitude Test verbal section over a standardized test of editorial skills.

Many of the descriptive procedures and measures described in the chapters in this book will yield scores that can be treated just like the scores obtained from standardized tests, but they are more valid in that they are based on actual pieces of writing, on some writer's real performance.

In deciding how to use these procedures and measures, one must have a comprehensive view of the various uses of evaluations and an understanding of certain important terms: *writing products, writing process, reliability,* and *validity.*

Writing evaluations have at least these uses:

Administrative
1 Predicting students' grades in English courses.
2 Placing or tracking students or exempting them from English courses.
3 Assigning public letter or number grades to particular pieces of writing and to students' work in an English course.

Instructional
4 Making an initial diagnosis of students' writing problems.
5 Guiding and focusing feedback to student writers as they progress through an English course.

Evaluation and Research
6 Measuring students' growth as writers over a specific time period.
7 Determining the effectiveness of a writing program or a writing teacher.
8 Measuring group differences in writing performance in comparison-group research.
9 Analyzing the performance of a writer chosen for a case study.
10 Describing the writing performance of individuals or groups in developmental studies, either cross-sectional or longitudinal in design.
11 Scoring writing in order to study possible correlates of writing performance.

Some of the measures described in this book will serve several of these uses, but some have quite limited and particular uses. For example, the most efficient measure for prediction or placement may not be the best measure for growth. The best measures for diagnosing a writer's performance at the beginning of a course will not necessarily be the best for determining amount of growth during the course, although the two sets of measures might overlap. Consequently, we think it is critical for teachers, researchers, and curriculum evaluators to know *why* they are evaluating before they choose measures and procedures.

Finally, we would like to offer definitions of the crucial terms for discussing evaluation.

Writing Products. Writing occurs in many different forms. Further, pieces in the same form can have quite different purposes or audiences, and the writer can be using different personae. When we talk about teaching writing or describing writing, we have to be very careful to include in *writing* all kinds of writing that people do out there in the world, not just the one or two kinds which are of traditional interest in secondary schools or colleges, like the essay about the literary work or the five paragraph theme. By *writing* we mean at least the following kinds of written discourse:

> *dramatic writing*
> > dialogues, scenes, short plays
> > Socratic dialogue
> > dramatic monologue
> > interior monologue
>
> *sensory recording*
>
> *reporting*
> > observational visit
> > interview
> > reporter-at-large
> > case study
> > profile
>
> *generalizing and theorizing*
> > essay about the literary work
> > expository essay on firsthand or researched information
>
> *research*
> > (from lower-order, primary documents; not from textbooks, summary articles, or encyclopedias)
>
> *personal writing*
> > journal, diary, log
> > commonplace book
> > personal letter
> > autobiography
> > firsthand biography
> > firsthand chronicle
>
> *poetry*
>
> *prose fiction*
>
> *business/practical*
> > personal resumé and job application
> > forms
> > technical reports
> > giving instructions
> > explaining a process
> > memo

business letter
    communicating technical information
    requesting information
    transmitting a report

Writing Process: Composing involves exploring and mulling over a subject; planning the particular piece (with or without notes or outline); getting started; making discoveries about feelings, values, or ideas, even while in the process of writing a draft; making continuous decisions about diction, syntax, and rhetoric in relation to the intended meaning and to the meaning taking shape; reviewing what has accumulated, and anticipating and rehearsing what comes next; tinkering and reformulating; stopping; contemplating the finished piece and perhaps, finally, revising. This complex, unpredictable, demanding activity is what we call the *writing process*. Engaging in it, we learn and grow. Measurement plans for instruction or research should not subvert it.

Reliability: If a measure or measurement scheme is reliable, it is fair to writers, permitting them to demonstrate what they can really do. For purposes of a quick tentative screening or placement decision, we need only ask a writer for one piece produced under the best conditions we can arrange. However, from previous research we know that either a comprehensive description of writing performance or a reliable rank ordering of a group of writers can be achieved only by asking for more than one piece of writing on more than one occasion and then involving two or more people in describing or rating each piece. Even then, we have reliable measurement of writing ability in only one mode. To test ability to write in different modes (personal narrative, explanation, dramatic dialogue, reportage, prose fiction) or to write for different purposes (explanation, persuasion, expression), we need multiple pieces on multiple occasions. As an example, we know from previous research that syntactic patterns vary from mode to mode, and further, that the best writers display the most variation.

Validity: If a measure or measurement scheme is valid, it does what we say it is doing. We want to insist on a careful distinction between *predictive validity* and two other kinds of validity, *content* and *construct validity*. If a measure has *predictive validity*, then it predicts performance at some time in the future or it correlates well with some criterion, say grades earned in English, or it permits an approximate grouping or placement. If a measure has *content validity*, then it is an appropriate measure for a particular writing program. It actually measures what writers have been practicing in a course or program. If a measure has *construct validity*, then it actually measures the construct of interest, in this case, writing ability or writing performance. We assume that teachers and researchers are primarily concerned with content and construct validity. Predictive validity is of interest primarily to makers of standardized tests.

About content validity we ask: Does a given measurement scheme really permit writers to demonstrate what they have achieved in a course or program?

About construct validity we ask: Does a given measurement scheme really permit a description of writing or the use of writing strategies? Is the scheme faithful to our best current information about the writing process, the writer's strategies, and the universe of written discourse?

We want to conclude by insisting that there is no mechanical or technical solution to the problems posed in evaluating writing. Since writing is an expressive human activity, we believe the best response to it is a receptive, sympathetic human response. We believe that each chapter in this book contributes to making that human response more insightful, more focused, more helpful.

Charles R. Cooper and Lee Odell

EVALUATING WRITING:
Describing, Measuring, Judging

In devising ways to measure students' growth in writing, we continually struggle with two problems: making judgments that are reliable, that we can reasonably assume are not idiosyncratic; and making judgments that are valid, that provide significant information about the writing we are dealing with. Holistic evaluation can offer a solution to both problems. There are, as Cooper points out in the following chapter, limits to the ways we can use some holistic procedures. Not all of them result in the sort of detailed description that we need for diagnosing students' writing problems. In addition, devising and using holistic evaluation procedures takes a good deal of time and effort. These limitations apart, however, it is possible to use existing procedures to conduct research or school-wide evaluation projects and to provide summative evaluations of students' writing. Moreover, as Cooper illustrates, it is possible for teachers in a given school to devise reliable, valid holistic procedures that are uniquely suited to their own school's writing program.

HOLISTIC EVALUATION OF WRITING

Charles R. Cooper

Introduction

Holistic evaluation of writing is a guided procedure for sorting or ranking written pieces. The rater takes a piece of writing and either (1) matches it with another piece in a graded series of pieces or (2) scores it for the prominence of certain features important to that kind of writing or (3) assigns it a letter or number grade. The placing, scoring, or grading occurs quickly, impressionistically, after the rater has practiced the procedure with other raters. The rater does not make corrections or revisions in the paper. Holistic evaluation is usually guided by a holistic scoring guide which describes each feature and identifies high, middle, and low quality levels for each feature.

Where there is commitment and time to do the work required to achieve reliability of judgment, holistic evaluation of writing remains the most valid and direct means of rank-ordering students by writing ability. Spending no more than two minutes on each paper, raters, guided by some of the holistic scoring guides I will describe here, can achieve a scoring reliability as high as .90 for individual writers. The scores provide a reliable rank-ordering of writers, an ordering which can then be used to make decisions about placement, special instruction, graduation, or grading.

For researchers and for state and national assessors, the possibilities in holistic evaluation are a reminder that they need not settle for frequency counts of word or sentence elements or for machine-scorable objective tests. A piece of writing communicates a whole message with a particular tone to a known audience for some purpose: information, argument, amusement, ridicule, titillation. At present, holistic evaluation by a human respondent gets us closer to what is essential in such a communication than frequency counts do.

3

Since holistic evaluation can be as reliable as multiple-choice testing and since it is always more valid, it should have first claim on our attention when we need scores to rank-order a group of students.

Overview of Various Types of Holistic Evaluation

Included here are brief descriptions of seven types of holistic evaluation: essay scale, analytic scale, dichotomous scale, feature analysis, primary trait scoring, general impression marking, and "center of gravity" response. Following these, I will focus on analytic scales, describing how they are constructed, presenting two in their entirety, and exploring their uses.

As my examples of holistic evaluation will illustrate, I am using the term "holistic" to mean any procedure which stops short of enumerating linguistic, rhetorical, or informational features of a piece of writing. Some holistic procedures may specify a number of particular features and even require that each feature be scored separately, but the reader is never required to stop and count or tally incidents of the feature. The reader uses the list of features only as a general guide—a set of reminders, a way of focusing—in reaching a holistic judgment. Readers who are familiar with the procedures used by the College Entrance Examination Board to score essays from the English Composition Test and Advance Placement Test in English will recognize that I am attempting to broaden somewhat the way we use the term "holistic." In the next chapter Lloyd-Jones labels as "atomistic" at least some of the types of holistic evaluation I describe below. Some uncertainty about terminology seems quite natural in an area in which the early research and field work has been so uncoordinated and in which we have not reached wide agreement on standard procedures.

Essay Scale

The essay scale is a series of complete pieces arranged according to quality. At one end of the series is an exemplary piece, at the other an inadequate one. The pieces which make up the scale are usually selected from large numbers of pieces written by students like those with whom the scale will be used. A rater attempts to place a new piece of writing along the scale, matching it with the scale piece most like it.

Perhaps the best-known essay scale in this country is one developed by a committee of the California Association of Teachers of English (Nail et al. 1960; and in Judine 1965) and now distributed by the National Council of Teachers of English. It was developed from an analysis and sorting of

561 essays written in California grade 12 classrooms on one of ten topics. The six papers in the published scale are on the topics juvenile delinquency, outdoor litter, rural life, and a favorite school subject. Each essay has been marked with correction symbols and with a few marginal notes. Following each essay is a "critical comment."

Another essay scale, *Assessing Compositions* (Martin et al. 1965), was developed by a committee of the London Association for the Teaching of English. It should be much better known than it is, although it, too, was distributed until recently by the National Council of Teachers of English. Presently, it is available only from the British publisher Blackie. Since it is a particularly sophisticated example of an essay scale, it deserves some detailed attention here.

While the California scale was developed for expository writing, the London scale was developed for "imaginative" writing from pieces written by fifteen-year-olds. The committee set one topic, "Alone," for a number of students in eight schools, but then filled out the final scale with pieces on other topics produced by the students in the regular writing program at the schools. Other topics are "Saying Goodbye," "Camping," "My Family," "A Walk Along the Cliff One Winter's Day at Sunset," "My First Dance," "My First Pop Performance," and "Our First Job." Altogether, the London scale includes twenty-eight pieces in groups of five to seven pieces of equivalent quality, with two additional outstanding pieces.

As the committee read and reread the pieces, they found they were using answers to the following questions to explain their general impressions of the quality of the pieces:

1 Does the experience seem real? Is there diversity of information in the detail, and is it relevant to the experience? Do the details show that the writer is recreating an experience or are they clichés?

2 Has something been made of the experience so that it has significance for writer and reader? Is the work structured? There may be a simple change of pace. There may be a sense of coming to the point in the narrative for which all before has prepared, and on which all that follows reflects.

3 Is the vocabulary precise and, where necessary, rich in associations? Is there sufficient variety and complexity of sentence structure to permit more complexity of subject, deeper understanding? Is the language being used in a personally creative way, or does one word so determine the next that there are only clichés of thought, feeling, and language?

4 Is there adequate control of spelling and punctuation so that the writer manages to communicate, and manages to do so without irritating the reader too much?

6 *Charles R. Cooper*

These questions suggest the possibility that the work being done on holistic evaluation can be useful to teachers and students who see the need for ways to guide and focus feedback in personal conferences or small-group writing workshops.

The main criteria for the grouping and ranking of the twenty-eight imaginative pieces of the London scale were:

1 Realization: the extent to which the writing directly reflects the writer's own experience (sincerity, spontaneity, vividness).
2 Comprehension: the extent to which a piece of writing shows an awareness of audience and can thereby be understood, permitting some concensus of response.
3 Organization: the extent to which a piece of writing has shape or coherence.
4 Density of Information: the amount of unique and significant detail.
5 Control of Written Language: extent of control over the special forms and patterns of written syntax and rhetoric.

The pieces are presented without critical marking or annotation. In a separate section of the pamphlet, each essay is discussed briefly in terms of the questions and criteria listed above. The discussions seem to me especially insightful in a number of ways, particularly in distinguishing between mere technical competence and effective communication. The raters have this to say about one essay: "The apparent competence of this essay masks its emptiness as a piece of writing . . . although there is an attempt at organization here, it is external to the meaning or experience of the [topic]. . . . The writer has not concentrated on the subject and its meaning but on performing a series of linguistic exercises whose connection with the subject is tenuous. . . . We think this notion of what good writing is can only hinder the development of children's ability to use the written language effectively."

Still another scale—and one designed for a purpose different from that of the California or London scales—is the Smith scale (V. Smith 1969). It assesses the accuracy of teacher judgment of elementary school writing. Teachers are given a set of five brief letters to a pen pal and asked to identify the two best and two worst. Scoring is based on the extent of teacher agreement with experts' rankings of the letters. Although Smith recommends the scale for acquainting teachers with the accuracy of their judgments and for screening composition raters in evaluation or research studies, a study by Whalen (1972) suggests the scale may be invalid for those purposes. At any rate, the Smith study does demonstrate another potential use for essay scales—measuring teacher agreement with experts and screening raters—and incidentally suggests a way to derive a score from such a scale.

Essay scales, then, have a number of uses. They can show student writers a range of quality for one particular writing task or writing mode; for example, the teacher could use a scale of five to eight pieces as the basis for a class discussion. An essay scale could be used to acquaint teachers-in-training with the range of writing quality at a particular grade level. In order to determine the range of writing abilities and as a basis for discussing the writing program, teachers in a school or at a particular grade level could cooperatively develop a scale. I would recommend that teachers develop a separate scale for each of the major types of writing in the writing program: explanation, personal narrative, reportage, prose fiction, to mention just four possibilities. Still another use for an essay scale is to set a standard, to draw a line of adequacy, indicating that all essays above some point on the scale would be acceptable in a college course, for high school graduation, for a "C" grade in a course, or for some other purpose.

During the 1920s and 1930s, essay scales were widely used by teachers and researchers (Braddock, Lloyd-Jones, and Schoer 1963), but I know of only one recent instance where an essay scale has been used as the writing-quality criterion measure in an experimental intervention study (Sanders and Littlefield 1975). As we shall see, other holistic schemes are more efficient and almost certainly more reliable.

Analytic Scale

An analytic scale, the holistic evaluation device of particular interest in this chapter, is a list of the prominent features or characteristics of writing in a particular mode. The list of features ordinarily ranges from four to ten or twelve, with each feature described in some detail and with high-mid-low points identified and described along a scoring line for each feature. Sometimes the high-mid-low points are exemplified with complete pieces of writing in the manner of an abbreviated essay scale.

To illustrate, here is a well-known scale (Diederich 1974) developed from an analysis of academics' and nonacademics' judgments of the writing of college freshmen.

	Low		Middle		High	
General Merit						
Ideas	2	4	6	8	10	
Organization	2	4	6	8	10	
Wording	1	2	3	4	5	
Flavor	1	2	3	4	5	_____
Mechanics						
Usage	1	2	3	4	5	
Punctuation	1	2	3	4	5	
Spelling	1	2	3	4	5	
Handwriting	1	2	3	4	5	_____
					Total	_____

The doubled values assigned to "ideas" and "organization" reflect the emphasis in the writing programs in the schools where the scale was initially used. The complete scale describes in a general way the high-mid-low points along each feature scoring line, as in the following description for "ideas":

> *High.* The student has given some thought to the topic and writes what he really thinks. He discusses each main point long enough to show clearly what he means. He supports each main point with arguments, examples, or details; he gives the reader some reason for believing it. His points are clearly related to the topic and to the main idea or impression he is trying to convey. No necessary points are overlooked and there is no padding.
>
> *Middle.* The paper gives the impression that the student does not really believe what he is writing or does not fully understand what it means. He tries to guess what the teacher wants, and writes what he thinks will get by. He does not explain his points very clearly or make them come alive to the reader. He writes what he thinks will sound good, not what he believes or knows.
>
> *Low.* It is either hard to tell what points the student is trying to make or else they are so silly that, if he had only stopped to think, he would have realized that they made no sense. He is only trying to get something down on paper. He does not explain his points; he only asserts them and then goes on to something else, or he repeats them in slightly different words. He does not bother to check his facts, and much of what he writes is obviously untrue. No one believes this sort of writing—not even the student who wrote it.

Readers learn to use the scale by studying the descriptions of high-mid-low values for each feature, trying the scale on pieces of student writing, and discussing the results.

I am merely introducing the analytic scale briefly in order to place it in the context of my overview of kinds of holistic evaluation. We will see later how analytic scales may be constructed, how they can provide reliable scores for placement or summative evaluation, and how they can be used to guide formative evaluation.

Dichotomous Scale

A dichotomous scale is a series of statements which can be answered yes or no. Instead of deciding on a score along a scoring line of five or ten points, as with the analytic scale, the rater simply decides whether the piece has the feature identified in the statement. Here is an example from a study of the effectiveness of community college writing programs. The scale was developed by the teachers participating in the study (Cohen, 1973).

	Score Sheet		
	Yes	No	
Content I.	_____	_____	1. Ideas themselves are insightful.
	_____	_____	2. Ideas are creative or original.
	_____	_____	3. Ideas are rational or logical.
	_____	_____	4. Ideas are expressed with clarity.
Organization II.	_____	_____	5. There is a thesis.
	_____	_____	6. Order of thesis idea is followed throughout the essay.
	_____	_____	7. Thesis is adequately developed.
	_____	_____	8. Every paragraph is relevant to the thesis.
	_____	_____	9. Each paragraph has a controlling idea.
	_____	_____	10. Each paragraph is developed with relevant and concrete details.
	_____	_____	11. The details that are included are well ordered.
Mechanics III.	_____	_____	12. There are many misspellings.
	_____	_____	13. There are serious punctuation errors.
	_____	_____	14. Punctuation errors are excessive.
	_____	_____	15. There are errors in the use of verbs.
	_____	_____	16. There are errors in use of pronouns.
	_____	_____	17. There are errors in use of modifiers.
	_____	_____	18. There are distracting errors in word usage.
	_____	_____	19. The sentences are awkward.

The *group* results from the study in which the scale was used demonstrated both that the writing programs in several colleges were having some effect on writing performance and that the placement of students into remedial and regular classes was reasonably accurate. No conventional reliability data are reported for the scale, since it was not being used to score individuals but only to compare group performance on a single pre- and posttest essay. The percentage of concurrence among all the raters on four essays distributed solely to gather reliability data ranged from .50 (a chance score on a dichotomous variable) to 1.00, but most of the percentages of concurrence for the nineteen items in the scale were in the seventies and eighties.

I doubt whether dichotomous scales would yield reliable scores on individuals, but for making gross distinctions between the quality of batches of essays, they seem quite promising, though apparently requiring no less time to use than an analytic scale for the same purpose.

Feature Analysis

Analytic and dichotomous scales are ordinarily quite comprehensive, attempting to direct the rater to several features in a piece of writing. By contrast, feature analysis focuses on a particular aspect of a piece, perhaps its structure. The one example I have of this type of holistic evaluation is an instrument developed by Stahl (1974) to describe the structural features of children's and adolescents' descriptions of their homes. It could probably be used with other descriptive writing tasks. No reliability data are included in the report.

The instrument has nine categories: indicated order, principle of selection, methods of arrangement, syntax, balance, organization, connectives, openings, and conclusion. Each of these categories can be scored for five types of structure. Let me illustrate by presenting here the complete description of the category *methods of arrangement*, which deals with "the manner in which the contents of the composition are arranged." The five types of structure for this category are arranged from most to least sophisticated.

Comprehensive. Explicit division of the rooms in a manner which clearly shows a general and comprehensive grasp of the subject. This division might be according to function (rooms used regularly for family living, nonessential convenience rooms such as a laundry room, or annexes such as a storeroom or veranda) or spatial position. This type includes every description which presents a kind of objective map (or which adds a map to the description, provided the description itself is "comprehensive" as defined).

Surveying. A description which presents the rooms and/or their contents by conducting a "tour" through the home. In order to classify a composition as being in this type, there must be clear signs in the language of the composition: words which describe, in different places within the composition, the movement through the home, or words which attempt to describe the precise relative positions of the furniture pieces within each room and the passing from one room to the next.

Associative. The order is dictated by verbal or sound associations which can be clearly demonstrated. There must be various definite instances of this in the composition, and its appearance must be conspicuous.

Egocentric. An arrangement which gives prominence to the writer's position: his point of view, the things which make an impression upon him, his feelings, his impressions, matters which affect him or belong to him (giving prominence to his room, his playthings).

Enumerating. Enumerating the things found in the home either by room (but without clear signs of a "survey") or without any discernible order. Here also are to be included those compositions in which different methods of arrangement are used at once without any one of them dominating, or which have no signs sufficient to classify them under one of the other methods of arrangement.

With this model teachers and researchers could develop feature analysis scales for any significant aspect of a particular kind of writing: voice and style of personal disclosure in autobiographical writing; structure or pattern in fictional prose; use of details and sensory images in writing up observations and interviews; presentation of speaker roles in dialogue and dramatic and interior monologue; use of classification and contrast to present information in exposition, to mention some possibilities.

Primary Trait Scoring

Primary Trait Scoring was developed for scoring the essays from the second (1974) writing assessment of the National Assessment of Educational Progress. (See the Lloyd-Jones chapter in this collection for a discussion of the development of Primary Trait Scoring and for an example of a Primary Trait Scoring Guide.) Like feature analysis and analytic scales, Primary Trait Scoring yields a score which can be quite reliable when raters are given careful training. Primary Trait Scoring guides focus the rater's attention on just those features of a piece which are relevant to the kind of discourse it is: to the special blend of audience, speaker role, purpose, and subject required by that kind of discourse and by the particular writing task. Furthermore, a unique quality of Primary Trait Scoring is that the scoring guides are constructed for a particular writing task set in a full rhetorical context. This close correspondence of rhetorically explicit task and holistic scoring guide is a new development in holistic evaluation of writing, a development almost certain to have great impact on the evaluation of writing. The correspondence permits a new precision in stating writing research hypotheses and in devising criterion measures for research and curriculum development. As a practical application of new rhetorical theories, Primary Trait Scoring will also very likely have an indirect impact on the way teachers give writing tasks and respond to them. Primary Trait Scoring is certainly the most sophisticated of the holistic evaluation schemes under review in this chapter and potentially the most useful.

General Impression Marking

General impression marking is the simplest of the procedures in this overview of types of holistic evaluation. It requires no detailed discussion of features and no summing of scores given to separate features. The rater simply scores the paper by deciding where the paper fits within the range of papers produced for that assignment or occasion. If the scores are to be used for ranking or for significance testing, raters must use the full range of scores available in order to approximate a normal score distribution. As this procedure has been developed by Education Testing Service and the College Entrance Examination Board to score the English Composition Test (Conlan 1976) and the Advanced Placement test in English (R. Smith 1975), raters must train themselves carefully—become "calibrated" to reach consensus—by reading and discussing large numbers of papers like those they will be scoring. (This procedure would be a requirement for obtaining reliable scores with any of the holistic schemes in this overview; I will discuss reliability problems later.) I should point out, however, that James Britton and his colleagues at the University of London Institute of Education (Britton, Martin, and Rosen 1966) have achieved reliabilities as high as .82 between teams of three raters who were experienced English teachers but who were given only minimal instructions, no training, and no chance to discuss among themselves—either within teams or between teams—the standards they would use for evaluating. The raters lived in different parts of England, received their instructions and the papers by mail, and were paid for their time.

At ETS raters use a scale of 1 to 4 to score the English Composition Test and a scale of 1 to 8 to score the Advanced Placement test. Holistic scoring in the first reports of the writing assessment of the National Assessment of Educational Progress (*Writing Mechanics* 1975) comes from a general impression marking on a scale of 1 to 8. Britton used a scale from 0 to 10.

General impression marking may be closer to analytic scale scoring than it seems at first. At the scoring of the Advanced Placement test, raters follow a "rubric" worked out in advance. The rubric is concerned mainly with the relevance of the answer to the essay question and with the content of the answer, rather than with general features of writing; but it does serve to focus a rater's reading of an essay in the way an analytic scale does. Even though raters scoring the English Composition Test have no rubric or feature list in hand, they have discussed sample papers at length. It is therefore not unreasonable to assume that they are using an implicit list of features or qualities to guide their judgments.

Center of Gravity Response

Peter Elbow's "center of gravity" response is intended not for scoring at all but for formative response and feedback. The reader reads the paper and then responds to the following:

a   First tell very quickly what you found to be the main points, main feelings, or centers of gravity. Just sort of say what comes to mind for fifteen seconds, for example, "Let's see, very sad; the death seemed to be the main event; um . . . but the joke she told was very prominent; lots of clothes."

b   Then summarize it into a single sentence.

c   Then choose one word from the writing which best summarizes it.

d   Then choose a word that isn't in the writing which best summarizes it. Do this informally. Don't plan or think too much about it. The point is to show the writer what things he or she made stand out most in your head, what shape the thing takes in your consciousness. This isn't a test to see whether you got the words right. It's a test to see whether the words got you right. Be sure to use different language from the language of the writing. This insures that the writer is getting it filtered through your perception and experience—not just parroted.

The Elbow scheme, which can be varied and adapted in many ways, has been used by teachers at several levels, junior high school through college. It exemplifies the best sort of formative response guide for students—a guide which directs them to something in each other's writings besides spelling and usage mistakes. An additional benefit is that it neatly precludes passing judgment on someone else's writing.

I include the Elbow scheme in order to broaden my review of holistic evaluation to encompass informal response guides that lead the reader to produce a response. From the teacher's or student's perspective, these will be more useful for teaching than any of the other guides I review above. A writer planning to revise a piece can certainly learn more from a dozen center of gravity responses from peers than from a dozen scores on an analytic scale, unless, of course, there is time to talk to the raters about why they scored the piece as they did. While I am interested in exploring the possibilities for teaching all kinds of holistic evaluation guides, my main concern in this chapter is to outline their uses for conventional measurement requirements: prediction of success in English, placement in special courses, and growth measurement. To use the current distinctions, I am more concerned in this chapter with summative than with formative evaluation.

Analytic Scales

Following this overview of several types of holistic evaluation, we come to a more detailed exploration of analytic scales. I want to show how they can be constructed and how they might be used in a variety of ways for evaluation and for teaching. I will also give some attention to the problems of achieving reliable ratings with analytic scales.

I recommend that researchers, teachers, and students construct analytic scales for use with the major kinds of writing commonly required or encouraged in schools. One advantage of analytic scales is that they can be developed for one kind of writing and then put to use thenceforth with all instances of that kind of writing, such as autobiographical incidents or essays about literary works. (See Moffett 1968 for a comprehensive list of kinds of writing. His list is based on notions of levels of abstraction in treating the subject and on rhetorical distance between writer and audience.) As useful as analytic scales can be for researchers and teachers (certainly they are an advance over using the Diederich expository scale with all kinds of writing), they do have some drawbacks. The main problem is that they are not sensitive to the variations in purpose, speaker role, and conception of audience which can occur in pieces written in the same mode. Current discourse theory persuades us that a piece of autobiographical incident, viewed as to its function or purpose, could be either expressive, persuasive, referential, or literary, that is, concerned primarily with self, other, subject, or language. While we must acknowledge, then, that analytic scales lack certain kinds of precision, we can still demonstrate their usefulness as general or global guides for responding to a piece of writing.

Developing an Analytic Scale

Procedures to follow in developing an analytic scale are simple though time-consuming. Since the features that make up the scale must be derived inductively from pieces of writing in the mode for which the scale is being constructed, the first requirement is for large amounts of writing of two kinds: published professional writing, and original student writing of varying quality. The second requirement is for critical, analytical, or theoretical treatises on the particular mode. In the case of personal narrative, the first scale to be illustrated below, we collect several dozen pieces of autobiography and firsthand biography (or memoir) from secondary school or college students on whose writing the scale will eventually be used. Then we obtain several recently published autobiographies and firsthand biographies, including collections of short pieces. While we're reading widely in the mode of personal narrative, we read a few pieces of criticism and theory, pieces on the nature of personal narrative as a mode of writing. As the reading progresses, we begin listing important features of personal narrative. If we are working with others on this project, we discuss our lists of features, shaping and modifying them as we try them out on pieces of student writing and examine the results. Gradually we evolve a list of features, comprehensive enough to include the key features of personal narrative but not so long that a rater-researcher or stu-

dent writer would find it unmanageable as a guide to scoring or responding.

When the list of features is established, we describe briefly in nontech-
nical language what we consider to be high, mid, and low quality levels
for each feature. These descriptions are helpful in "anchoring" the points
along a scoring line.

These procedures were the ones followed by four Buffalo-area English
teachers—Greg Anderson, Dale Kaiser, Nathalie Ketterer, and Donald
McAndrew—and this writer in developing Personal Narrative Writing
Scales (PNWS). The PNWS is intended for use either by high school students themselves or by teachers and researchers who would be rating
high school students' papers in this mode. The PNWS is designed for use
with both autobiography and firsthand biography, but scales could also
be developed for each separately. It can be found in its entirety in Appendix A.

After practice on several papers using the complete scale as a guide,
and after inter-rater reliability checks in the instance of a research or curriculum evaluation study, raters can score papers using either the analytic
scale or the dichotomous scale.

There is another scale, a quite different one solely for use with dramatic
writing, developed in the same manner as the PNWS. This writer and the
following Buffalo-area teachers developed Dramatic Writing Scales
(DWS): Molly Brannigan, Tom Callaghan, Ann Feldman, Rosemary
Gates, Warren Hoffman, and Thomas MacLennan. The DWS can be
found in Appendix B.

Both the PNWS and the DWS could have been developed by teacher or
researcher groups anywhere. They can certainly be modified and improved. While both have been used extensively in classrooms by students
to guide peer feedback, neither has been used in a research study. Consequently, we do not have rater reliability data to report from the scales.
However, since both conform in format and general approach to several
current scales which have been used with high reliability in research studies, we are confident the same results can be achieved with PNWS and
DWS.

Uses for Analytic Scales

The PNWS and DWS and others like them (see Fagan, Cooper, and
Jensen 1975 for a review of several analytic scales) have a variety of uses,
some of them already suggested in this chapter. Where a reliable score
is needed for a student—a score representing his or her writing performance at one point in time, relative to the performance of other students'
writing at the same time on the same topic or topics—an analytic scale

will guide and focus raters' scoring, insuring enough agreement to permit a reliable score to come from summed multiple ratings (see discussion of reliability below). This score can be used for any purpose to which scores are ordinarily put in education: prediction, placement, exemption, growth measurement, program evaluation, or experimental or correlational research. The importance of such a score for writing teachers and researchers is that it is a *valid* score, obtained from actual writing and not from a multiple-choice test of presumed writing skills.

Let's conjecture about what use a high school English department might make of such a score. A score for each student based on the same set of writing tasks given on special school-wide writing days (Diederich 1974; Cooper 1975) permits a rank-ordering of the entire student body and of each grade level. Therefore, we know precisely where a tenth-grader named Susanna stands as a writer in relation to all the students in the school (grades 10–12) and to the students in her grade level. We have a great deal of confidence in Susanna's relative placement because the task we set was valid (we actually asked her to write whole pieces of discourse) and the rating or scoring was reliable (we followed procedures to be outlined below and we computed the reliability of the ratings). This score won't tell us anything we need to know to improve Susanna's writing, and so it is quite limited information in the context of the whole writing program, but it is useful nevertheless. For example, we may learn that Susanna is one of the dozen or so best writers in the tenth-grade class, and a better writer than three-fourths of the seniors. Where writing is an important part of the English program, and where students are tracked by ability, we have an important piece of information to pass along to the counselor who plans Susanna's program. Certainly we can make a confident decision about placing Susanna in a small honors section or in an Advance Placement class.

But let's assume students are not tracked and that each teacher is interested in forming heterogeneous small-group writing workshops early in the year. The teacher will know exactly who the six best writers are, Susanna among them, in the class of thirty. One of the six will go into each of the five-member workshops. These six best writers could also, at least occasionally, meet together as a workshop. Of course, the teacher can get an approximate ranking of the class after seeing the first few pieces of writing from the group, but the school-wide ranking may save time in forming workshop groups or planning other class activities, and it has the additional advantage of being objective, of being based on a cooperative and unbiased assessment of each student's writing performance.

What else can we do with Susanna's score? We could pair her with the lowest-ranked student in the class in a tutoring relationship. We could ask her to tutor for pay or for extra credit in the English department's "writing place," where students from anywhere in the school come for help with their reports and papers. We could make it easy for her to volunteer to spend an hour or two a week in a nearby elementary school or middle school, assisting a teacher in the writing program. Perhaps the journalism teacher would want to know about Susanna's ranking, or the English teacher sponsoring a Foxfire-type journal, or the history teacher planning a large-scale, cooperative, student-written history of the school or the community.

But what if Susanna had been among the dozen or so lowest-ranked tenth-grade writers? There she is, right at the bottom of the list—rather difficult to ignore. We know she will need special help. If we get the school-wide ranking each year, we will know at the end of Grade 11 whether Susanna remains at the bottom of the ranking. In that case we can arrange special instruction for her during her senior year.

This reliable ranking of all students by writing performance also has important public-relations benefits (Cooper 1975). Successive rankings permit the English department to demonstrate that, as a group, students improve as writers during their three years; Susanna's rank will move up through the whole student body (grades 10–12) during her three years in high school, even though her rank might remain the same within her own class.

For program evaluation or for research on methods of teaching writing, an analytic scale can serve as a guide to raters choosing the better of each student's paired pre- and post-essays on matched topics of the same kind of discourse (O'Hare 1973; Odell 1976). Where a criterion measure is required in a research study, raters can use an analytic scale to score each student's writings.

At the college level there is a need for information about writing performance in order to make decisions about placement, exemption, or certification. Where college faculty will not use standardized tests because they consider them invalid, analytic scales can guide raters' judgments about actual writing produced by students. The rank-ordering obtained from a test day can do everything that standardized equivalency tests will do. Appropriate local cut-off points in the ranking can be established in order to determine which students may be exempt from courses or which students should be assigned to courses of varying difficulty levels. (In making these comments I do not want to seem to be supporting examination by equivalency testing. My own view is that anyone can profit from a good writing course anytime. For me, the question is not whether we should exempt or who we should exempt, but how soon all of us are going to start teaching writing as competently as the best writing teachers in this country, teachers who regularly describe for us in detail how they go about it.)

So far I have discussed analytic scales as they are used to guide the acquisition of reliable scores for writers, scores which can then be used in all the ways we have learned in the last few decades to use normally distributed or rank-ordered scores. Now let me discuss some more informal uses within the classroom. With the scoring apparatus and the high-mid-low distinctions removed, the PNWS and the DWS can be helpful guides to formative evaluation, to feedback and response to each piece the writer produces. Such a guide for student use could include the list of features in either scale, the short descriptions of each feature, and the description of the "high" level of each feature, perhaps with the statements rephrased as questions for the reader to ask the writer or to ask of the writer's piece. In this regard, the dichotomous scales following both PNWS and DWS can be helpful; with the statements rephrased as questions, the scales can be used like checklists during the editing and revising stages.

Elsewhere in this collection, Mary Beaven explores the possibilities for training students to use such guides and checklists for self-evaluation and peer evaluation. At least two researchers (Alpren 1973; Sager 1973) report that the quality of writing from upper elementary school students improves when they receive guided teacher or peer feedback from analytic scales.

The Reliability Problem in Holistic Evaluation

We all know how unreliable ratings of essays can be: a group of raters will assign widely varying grades to the same essay. This phenomenon has been demonstrated repeatedly for decades. It is an incontrovertible empirical fact. You or I could demonstrate it tomorrow in a simple experiment. People who write and sell standardized, multiple-choice tests have used this fact to argue that we can get a reliable writing score from students only if we give them standardized tests, or at least give one in conjunction with a writing sample and then add the scores from each.

Curiously, another fact that often is ignored or slighted in discussions of the unreliability of essay grades is that we have known for almost as long as we have known about unreliability that reliability can be improved to an acceptable level *when raters from similar backgrounds are carefully trained*. In 1934 a researcher demonstrated that rater reliability could be improved from a range of .30 to .75 before training to a range of .73 to .98 after training (Stalnaker 1934). (A reliability coefficient of .80 is considered high enough for program evaluation, a reliability of .90 for individual growth measurement in teaching or research [Diederich 1974].) A more recent study (Follman and Anderson 1967) reports reliabilities for five raters ranging from .81 to .95 on five different types of holistic evaluation. Another recent study (Moslemi 1975) reports a reliability of .95 for three raters scoring "creative" writing. In a school-district curriculum evaluation study just completed here at Buffalo, Lee Odell obtained agreements between two raters of 80%, 100%, and 100% in choosing the better essay in each of thirty pairs of pre/posttest essays, in each of three kinds of writing. The raters, both experienced teachers and graduate students in English education, spent an average of an hour of training time preparing to judge each kind of writing.

As emphatically as I can, then, let me correct the record about the reliability of holistic judgments: *When raters are from similar backgrounds and when they are trained with a holistic scoring guide—either one they borrow or devise for themselves on the spot—they can achieve nearly perfect agreement in choosing the better of a pair of essays; and they can achieve scoring reliabilities in the high eighties and low nineties on their summed scores from multiple pieces of a student's writing.* Let me bring up some support. In a study of the reliability of grading essays, Follman and Anderson (1967) conclude:

> It may now be suggested that the unreliability usually obtained in the evaluation of essays occurs primarily because raters are to a considerable degree heterogeneous in academic background and have had different experiential backgrounds which are likely to produce different attitudes and values which operate significantly in their evaluations of essays. The function of a theme evaluation procedure, then, becomes that of a sensitizer or organizer of the rater's perception and gives direction to his attitudes and values; in other words, it points out what he should look for and guides his judgment.

Further assurance comes from Coffman (1971): "In general, when made aware of discrepancies, teachers tend to move their own ratings in the direction of the average ratings of the group. Over a period of time, the ratings of the staff as a group tend to become more reliable."

And now we come to the main constraints on achieving reliable scores of writing performance: cooperation and time. Reliabilities as high as the ones I mention above are never possible from one rating of one paper. Why? Writers vary in their performance, and raters disagree, even when they are alike and have been trained carefully. To overcome these difficulties we must have at least two pieces of a student's writing, preferably written on different days; and we must have at least two independent ratings of each piece. Further, we must permit the student to give us his or her best rehearsed or researched performance under controlled conditions to insure that the student actually does the writing him or herself even though he or she may be using notes (see Sanders and Littlefield 1975 for procedures for obtaining rehearsed writing). Finally, there are theoretical reasons to believe that the writing task we set for the students should specify a speaker role, audience, and purpose (see the Lloyd-Jones chapter).

The raters themselves must be carefully trained. They should practice using the holistic scoring guide with sample papers exactly like those they will be scoring, and they must be able to make their judgments within the context of the range of performances in the particular set of papers they are scoring. Scoring is always relative to the set of papers at hand and must take account of the writing task, the conditions under which the writing was done, the age and ability of the students, and the full range of quality of the papers. Reliability cannot be achieved when some raters are using an absolute standard of quality, perhaps that of published adult writing. Some papers must receive the highest scores, some the lowest, and most the scores in the middle range. Raters should check the reliability of their ratings during training to insure they reach an acceptable level before they begin the actual scoring. Then once the scoring is underway, they should periodically check themselves on perhaps every twenty-fifth paper (Diederich 1974 offers simple procedures for determining reliabilities).

Over the last few years several researchers have thoroughly explored the causes of variation in writing performance and rater judgments, and summaries of this research are available (Braddock, Lloyd-Jones, and Schoer 1963; McColly 1970; Britton, Martin, and Rosen 1966). At the same time, several writers have worked out in some detail ways we can adequately overcome these problems (Diederich 1974; Cooper 1975; Sanders and Littlefield 1975). Consequently, where there is commitment to valid measurement of writing performance, it can be achieved.

Conclusion

In this chapter I have reviewed various types of holistic evaluation of writing and have discussed at some length one kind of holistic evaluation, the analytic scale. Already widely used by teachers and researchers, it can be put to much more sophisticated and comprehensive uses than it has been; and I have proposed a number of refinements and uses at various levels of measurement and evaluation. Whether we need scores for prediction, placement, exemption, or growth measurement, or whether we need a guide to informal diagnosis or feedback, analytic scales can be useful. Most important, when we need scores, we can be confident we are obtaining them in a valid way, from human responses to actual pieces of writing.

There is, of course, a serious reliability problem. To overcome it, groups of teachers or researchers have to work together to train themselves as raters. They have to cooperate further to obtain multiple independent ratings of at least two pieces of a student's writing. And they have to be willing to spend the time required to do this work: two ratings of each paper written by 1500 high school students require 100 hours of rating time. As large as a time requirement of 100 hours seems, it serves mainly to remind us how much time secondary school and college English teachers regularly spend reading student papers. The holistic rating procedures I am recommending require no more than two minutes per paper, an amount of time far less than teachers ordinarily spend responding to a paper during the writing course. What we gain from the time we spend rating papers is a valid normative measure of a student's writing performance.

Even if we are not concerned with obtaining reliable scores, we can still put analytic scales to use in the classroom. They provide a public statement of the general features of writing stressed in a writing course, and they provide a focus for students' examination of their own writing and the writing of others. They insure that any response to writing will be appropriate to its type, reasonably comprehensive, and concerned, at least in part, with substantive matters.

Appendix A: Personal Narrative Writing Scales

1. General Qualities:

    A. Author's Role

    The author's role is the relationship of the author to the subject, incident, or person. In *autobiography* the author writes about himself/herself. He/she is the main participant. Most of the time he/she will use the pronouns, I, me, we, us. In *biography* the author writes about some other person. He/she is not involved in what happens; he/she is just an observer. He/she uses the pronouns, he, she, him, her, it, they, them.

    High   The author keeps his/her correct role of either participant or observer throughout.

    Middle   In autobiography, a few noticeable distracting times the author talks too much about another person's actions; or, in biography, he/she talks too much about his/her own actions.

    Low   The author talks about himself/herself or others as participant or observer anytime he/she pleases so that you can barely tell whether it is supposed to be autobiography or biography. There is confusion as to author's role. He/she is not consistently either observer or participant.

B. Style or Voice

High   The author states what he/she really thinks and feels. Expressing personal experiences, the writer comes through as an individual, and his/her work seems like his/hers and his/hers alone. The voice we hear in the piece really interests us.

Middle The author uses generalizations or abstract language, seldom including personal details and comments. While the piece may be correct, it lacks the personal touch. The voice seems bland, careful, a little flat, and not very interesting.

Low   We don't really hear a recognizable voice in the piece. The style seems flat and lifeless.

C. Central Figure
    Details about the central figure make him/her seem "real." The character is described physically and as a person.

High   The central figure is described in such detail that he/she is always "real" for you.

Middle The central character can be "seen," but is not as real as he/she could be.

Low   The central character is not a real living person; he/she is just a name on a page. You cannot see him/her or understand him/her.

D. Background
    The setting of the action is detailed so that it seems to give the events a "real" place in which to happen.

High   The action occurs in a well-detailed place that you can almost see.

Middle Sometimes the setting seems vivid and real; but sometimes the action is just happening, and you are not really aware of what the setting is.

Low   The action occurs without any detailed setting. You see the action, but you cannot see it in a certain place.

E. Sequence
    The order of events is clear, giving the reader a precise view of the sequence of incidents.

High   The order of events is always clear to you even if at times the author might talk about the past or the future.

Middle A few times it is not clear which event happened first.

Low   You really cannot figure out which event comes first or goes after any other event.

F. Theme
    The author chooses the incidents and details for some reason. There

seems to be some purpose behind the choice of subject matter, some *theme* holding it all together and relating the parts to the whole. There seems to be a point to it.

High The importance of the author's subject is either directly explained to you or it is implied in a way that makes it clear.

Middle You can see why the author's subject is important to him/her, but it is not as clearly stated or implied as it could be.

Low You cannot figure out why the subject is important to the author.

II. Diction, Syntax, and Mechanics

    A. Wording

        High Words are employed in a unique and interesting way. While some of the language might be inappropriate, the author seems thoughtful and imaginative.

        Middle Common, ordinary words are used in the same old way. The paper has some trite, over-worked expressions. The author, on the other hand, may work so hard at being different that he/she sounds like a talking dictionary, in which case he/she, also, merits this rating.

        Low The word choice is limited and immature. Sometimes words are even used incorrectly—the wrong word is used.

    B. Syntax

        High The sentences are varied in length and structure. The author shows a confident control of sentence structure. The paper reads smoothly from sentence to sentence. There are no run-together sentences or sentence fragments.

        Middle The author shows some control of sentence structure and only occasionally writes a sentence which is awkward or puzzling. Almost no run-ons and fragments.

        Low Many problems with sentence structure. Sentences are short and simple in structure, somewhat childlike and repetitious in their patterns. There may be run-ons and fragments.

    C. Usage

        High There are no obvious errors in usage. The author shows he/she is familiar with the standards of edited written English.

        Middle A few errors in usage appear in the paper, showing the author has not quite been consistent in using standard forms.

        Low The writing is full of usage errors.

D. Punctuation

    High   The author consistently uses appropriate punctuation.

    Middle Most of the time the writer punctuates correctly.

    Low   The writing contains many punctuation errors.

E. Spelling

    High   All words are spelled correctly.

    Middle A few words are misspelled.

    Low   Many words are misspelled.

Analytic Scale

Reader_____ Paper_____

	Low		Middle		High
I. General Qualities:					
A. Author's Role	2	4	6	8	10
B. Style or Voice	2	4	6	8	10
C. Central Figure	2	4	6	8	10
D. Background	2	4	6	8	10
E. Sequence	2	4	6	8	10
F. Theme	2	4	6	8	10
II. Diction, Syntax, and Mechanics:					
A. Wording	1	2	3	4	5
B. Syntax	1	2	3	4	5
C. Usage	1	2	3	4	5
D. Punctuation	1	2	3	4	5
E. Spelling	1	2	3	4	5

Total _____

Dichotomous Scale

Reader_____ Paper_____

	YES	NO	
I.	_____	_____	Author's role consistent
	_____	_____	Interesting personal voice
	_____	_____	Theme clearly presented
	_____	_____	Background rich and supportive
	_____	_____	Sequence of events clear
	_____	_____	Central figure fully developed
II.	_____	_____	Wording unique and developed
	_____	_____	Syntax correct and varied
	_____	_____	Usage errors few
	_____	_____	Punctuation errors few
	_____	_____	Spelling errors few

Total   Yes_____

Appendix B: Dramatic Writing Scales

The language of dramatic writing is different from other types of writing because it is meant to be heard. We expect the language to be in the present tense because the events unfold as we watch and listen. Another special aspect of the language of dramatic writing is that there is no narrator or voice to tell us of descriptions and histories. In dramatic language this information is hidden in the face-to-face, ongoing conversations of the characters. While each character speaks, other tenses than the present are used to talk to other characters. For example, one character may relate to another a past series of events leading to the present situation. The stage directions give hints to the actors concerning their actions and tone of voice, which the narrator would otherwise tell about in a descriptive section of prose.

I. Language Factors

A. Conversation: Realism
   Does the conversation sound realistic?

   High The characters' conversations go on as if you were eavesdropping (secretly listening) to their talk. Everything that is said is very clear to you.

   Middle The characters' conversation sometimes leaves out something important. Almost everything that is said is clear to you.

   Low The characters' conversation leaves out so much that you have trouble understanding what is said.

B. Conversation: Situation
   Does the way the characters talk match the situation they are in?

   High The characters talk exactly as you would expect in the situation.

   Middle The characters talk as you expect in the situation most of the time.

   Low The characters do not talk as you would expect in the situation.

C. Stage Directions
   If stage directions are used, are they short and clear?

   High The stage directions tell the actors how to act and speak when you cannot decide from the characters' talk.

   Middle The stage directions tell the actors how to act and speak most of the time. Sometimes they leave information out or repeat information.

   Low The stage directions confuse the actors about how to act and speak.

II. Shape Factors

    A. Beginning

Does reading the opening lines of this dramatic writing make you want to continue? Do they make you feel that what follows will be interesting?

High   I am intrigued by the beginning. It seems interesting and makes me want to continue the reading.

Middle   The beginning is interesting; however, I have seen this beginning used before. It's not all that unusual.

Low   The beginning is not particularly interesting. It gets the dramatic writing off to a slow start.

    B. Structure

Structure refers to the way this dramatic writing is built, or put together, with a beginning, middle, and end. It has to do with the way the parts fit together, the overall design which reveals the problem and how that problem is solved.

High   The elements of the dramatic writing are tied together in an interesting, well-organized manner. There is a good deal of detail and a resolution that is believable.

Middle   Although there is some attempt at proceeding from beginning to end in an organized manner, you are unsatisfied. This could be due either to a "forced" conclusion to the writing or to the writer's failure to tie all the elements together very successfully.

Low   The sequence of events is confused, rambling, not well-organized. Very little detail is given.

    C. Ending

The ending is the dramatic writing's conclusion. It is reached *after* a problem has been resolved.

High   The ending follows sensibly from the story, is unique, very well stated, and, possibly, is a surprise ending.

Middle   The ending makes sense to the dramatic writing but is not very unique or unusual.

Low   Very ordinary and usual. The ending is just what you expected and does not surprise you. It may not resolve the problem posed in the writing, or it may not resolve it in a believable manner.

III. Characterization Factors

Having characters that are well-developed and real to the readers is an important part of dramatic writing. Making the reader understand how and why the characters act the way they do will give the reader a more personal and interesting view of the entire dramatic piece.

A. Development and Credibility

All the characters in the writing should be as much like real people as possible. The reader should be able to see the difference between the major and minor characters. Major characters (the important ones) should be more fully developed. The reader should know a lot about them. They should see him/her acting and reacting in many different situations. Minor characters (less important ones) also have to be realistic, but the reader doesn't have to know as much about them.

High   All major characters seem to be like real people. Each character is a different person, and the reader has no problem telling which character is which. Minor characters are also real, but they aren't as detailed as major ones. The writer tells the reader much about his characters through dialogue. Narration is kept to a minimum.

Middle   Not all the characters seem like real people, all the time. Sometimes they do things that real people probably wouldn't do. The reader has a hard time telling which characters are which. They all seem alike.

Low   Little about the characters seems real. They act in ways which most people wouldn't. There is no difference between major and minor characters. The characters are almost entirely described by narration, with little use of dialogue.

B. Consistency

The characters seem like the same people throughout the piece of writing. Their emotions might change (they may change by laughing, crying, feeling happy or sad, etc.), but their basic personalities will remain the same. (A boy who was very stingy with his money at the beginning of the story wouldn't suddenly start giving money away for no reason.)

High   All the characters remain the same throughout the piece. Their personalities do not change. If there is a basic change, a reason is given for it in the dialogue.

Middle   The characters do not always seem like the same people. There are times when they do things that don't seem to fit.

Low   The characters' personalities are constantly changing. The reader never knows what to expect from them.

IV. Mechanics Factors

A. Dramatic Form

Dramatic Form refers to the physical arrangement of words on the paper. Is the physical form of the paper such that the reader wants to continue reading? The names of the characters should come before their lines, and be set off to the left, followed by a colon. If stage directions are used, they should be enclosed in parentheses.

High   The form is nearly perfect; stage directions are set off by parentheses.

Middle   There are a few errors in form or occasionally confusing stage directions.

Low   The paper contains many errors in dramatic form: characters' names are omitted or put in the wrong places. Stage directions are run into the characters' lines.

B.   Spelling
  Dialect spellings are permitted in dramatic writing. Where they are used, they should be consistent so that the actor would have no difficulty reading the character's lines.

High   All words are spelled correctly, even the most difficult words. Dialect spellings are consistent.

Middle   Only a few words are misspelled. Dialect spellings are mostly consistent.

Low   There are many misspellings, even of very ordinary words. Dialect spellings are inconsistent.

C.   End Punctuation

High   End punctuation occurs at natural places, thus making the dialogue easy to follow.

Middle   There are only a few errors in end punctuation, without making the dialogue difficult to follow.

Low   End punctuation marks are either not present or are placed so that often the dialogue is hard to follow.

V.   Response Factors
  Rather than focusing your attention on one aspect of drama, in this section of the scale you will be asked to assess the dramatic work as a whole. The questions under this heading of the scale will probably be the easiest for you to answer because you know what you like and dislike. However, you should try to use your answers to these questions as guides in answering the other more specific questions. For example, if you really enjoyed a work, try to decide what aspect of the work made it so successful.

A.   Entertainment

High   I felt the work was very entertaining.

Middle   I was only mildly entertained by the work as a whole.

Low   The work was not entertaining.

B.   Originality

High   The work made me think about something in a way that I hadn't previously considered.

Middle   While there were some moments of originality in the work, there were a lot of ideas I had heard before.

Low   There was nothing new in this work.

Reader Score Sheet

DIRECTIONS: For each quality listed below, circle the number that most nearly describes the position of this paper on the following scale from high to low.

LANGUAGE FACTORS	*HIGH*		*MIDDLE*		*LOW*
I.1 Conversation – Realism..........	5	4	3	2	1
I.2 Conversation – Situation.........	5	4	3	2	1
I.3 Stage Directions................	5	4	3	2	1

TOTAL LANGUAGE SCORE: _____

SHAPE FACTORS					
II.1 Beginning.....................	5	4	3	2	1
II.2 Structure......................	5	4	3	2	1
II.3 Ending........................	5	4	3	2	1

TOTAL SHAPE SCORE: _____

CHARACTERIZATION FACTORS					
III.1 Development..................	5	4	3	2	1
III.2 Consistency..................	5	4	3	2	1

TOTAL CHARACTERIZATION SCORE: _____

MECHANICS FACTORS					
IV.1 Dramatic Form................	5	4	3	2	1
IV.2 Spelling.......................	5	4	3	2	1
IV.3 Punctuation..................	5	4	3	2	1

TOTAL MECHANICS SCORE: _____

RESPONSE FACTORS					
V.1 Entertainment.................	5	4	3	2	1
V.2 Originality....................	5	4	3	2	1

TOTAL RESPONSE SCORE: _____

TOTAL SCORE: _____

Dichotomous Scale

	YES	NO	
LANGUAGE	——	——	1. Conversation sounds realistic.
	——	——	2. Characters' talk fits the situation.
	——	——	3. There are stage directions.
	——	——	4. Stage directions are clear.
SHAPE	——	——	5. Opening lines are interesting.
	——	——	6. There is a definite beginning.
	——	——	7. There is a definite ending.
	——	——	8. The ending is interesting.
CHARACTERIZATION	——	——	9. The characters seem real.
	——	——	10. The characters are consistent.
MECHANICS	——	——	11. The form is consistent.
	——	——	12. Spelling rules are observed.
	——	——	13. Punctuation rules are observed.
RESPONSE	——	——	14. The work is entertaining.
	——	——	15. The work made me think about something in a way I hadn't previously considered.
Totals:	——	——	

Bibliography

Alpren, Patricia F. "Can Children Be Helped to Increase the Originality of Their Story Writing?" *Research in the Teaching of English* 7 (1973):372–86.

Braddock, Richard; Lloyd-Jones, Richard; and Schoer, Lowell. *Research in Written Composition.* Urbana, Ill.: National Council of Teachers of English, 1963.

Britton, James N.; Martin, Nancy C.; and Rosen, Harold. *Multiple Marking of Compositions.* London: Her Majesty's Stationery Office, 1966.

Chomsky, Noam. *Aspects of the Theory of Syntax.* Cambridge, Mass.: MIT Press, 1969.

Coffman, William E. "On the Reliability of Ratings of Essay Examinations in English." *Research in the Teaching of English* 5 (1971):24-36.

Cohen, Arthur M. "Assessing College Students' Ability to Write Compositions." *Research in the Teaching of English* 7 (1973):356-71.

Conlan, Gertrude. *How the Essay in the CEEB English Test is Scored.* Princeton, N. J.: Educational Testing Service, 1976.

Cooper, Charles R. "Measuring Growth in Writing." *English Journal* 64 (March 1975):111-20.

Diederich, Paul B. *Measuring Growth in English.* Urbana, Ill.: National Council of Teachers of English, 1974.

Elbow, Peter. *Writing without Teachers.* New York: Oxford University Press, 1973.

Fagan, William T.; Cooper, Charles R.; and Jensen, Julie M. *Measures for Research and Evaluation in the English Language Arts.* Urbana, Ill.: National Council of Teachers of English, 1975.

Follman, John C., and Anderson, James A. "An Investigation of the Reliability of Five Procedures for Grading English Themes." *Research in the Teaching of English* 1 (1967):190-200.

Judine, Sister, I. H. M., ed. *A Guide for Evaluating Student Composition.* Urbana, Ill.: National Council of Teachers of English, 1965.

Martin, N. C., et al. *Assessing Compositions.* Glasgow: Blackie, 1965.

McColly, William. "What Does Educational Research Say About the Judging of Writing Ability?" *The Journal of Educational Research* 64 (1970):148-56.

Moffett, James. *A Student-Centered Language Arts Curriculum, Grades K-13: A Handbook for Teachers.* Boston: Houghton Mifflin, 1968.

Moslemi, Marlene H. "The Grading of Creative Writing Essays." *Research in the Teaching of English* 9 (1975): 154-61.

Nail, Pat; Fitch, Rodney; Halverson, John; Grant, Phil; and Winn, N. Field. *A Scale for Evaluation of High School Student Essays.* Urbana, Ill.: National Council of Teachers of English, 1960.

National Assessment of Educational Progress. *Writing Mechanics, 1969-74: A Capsule Description of Changes in Writing Mechanics.* Denver: National Assessment of Educational Progress, 1975.

Odell, Lee. "The Classroom Teacher as Researcher." *English Journal* 65 (January 1976):106-11.

O'Hare, Frank. *Sentence Combining: Improving Student Writing without Formal Grammar Instruction.* NCTE Research Report, no. 15. Urbana, Ill.: National Council of Teachers of English, 1973.

Sager, Carol. *Improving the Quality of Written Composition through Pupil Use of Rating Scale.* Ann Arbor, Mich.: University Microfilms, 1973. Order no. 73-23 605.

Sanders, Sara E., and Littlefield, John H. "Perhaps Test Essays Can Reflect Significant Improvement in Freshman Composition: Report on a Successful Attempt." *Research in the Teaching of English* 9 (1975): 145-53.

Smith, Ruth. *Grading the Advanced Placement English Examination.* Princeton, N. J.: College Board Publications, 1975.

Smith, Vernon H. "Measuring Teacher Judgment in the Evaluation of Written Composition." *Research in the Teaching of English* 3 (1969):181-95.

Stahl, Abraham. "Structural Analysis of Children's Compositions." *Research in the Teaching of English* 8 (1974):184-205.

Stalnaker, John M. "The Construction and Results of a Twelve-Hour Test in English Composition." *School and Society* 39 (1934):218-24.

Whalen, Thomas E. "A Validation of the Smith Test for Measuring Teacher Judgment of Written Composition." *Education* 93 (November 1972):172-75.

Although originally developed as a means of surveying the writing ability of large numbers of students, Primary Trait Scoring procedures can be used for several purposes. They can be used to make summative evaluations of students' writing and to generate numerical data for research studies and curriculum evaluation projects, but they also provide a detailed, precise description of students' performances on a specific rhetorical task. Teachers can use this description as a diagnosis of students' writing abilities and as a means of providing students with formative evaluation. Primary Trait Scoring is not concerned with qualities of writing—syntactic fluency, for example—that are presumed to be characteristic of *all* good writing. Rather, it asks readers to determine whether a piece of writing has certain characteristics or primary traits that are crucial to success with a given rhetorical task. Based on a carefully worked-out theory of discourse which can provide a valid and reliable picture of students' writing, Primary Trait Scoring is one of the most promising alternatives to standardized, multiple-choice tests of writing.

PRIMARY TRAIT SCORING

Richard Lloyd-Jones

In discussing tests of writing ability, one should have in mind a working definition of "writing," since that term is used equivocally to refer to any part of the large range between "handwriting" and "great literary works." Here, "writing" is synonymous with "discourse." And discourse will be discussed in terms of its *aims*, which relate to the functions of language, and in terms of its *features*, which are the separate elements, devices, and mechanisms of language. Judgments about the quality of writing are—or should be—primarily related to aims (i.e., does the piece of writing fulfill its purpose?). Yet to be informative about those judgments one must be able to describe the writing in terms of its features (e.g., the level of vocabulary).

Tests of writing ability are either *atomistic* or *holistic*. Atomistic tests rely on the assessment of particular features associated with skill in discoursing, whereas holistic tests consider samples of discourse only as whole entities. Holistic tests are of two kinds: those that deal with a piece of writing as representative of all discourse (such as the method perfected by the Educational Testing Service) or those that isolate subcategories of the universe of discourse and rate writing samples in terms of their aptness within the prescribed range (such as the Primary Trait Scoring method as developed by the National Assessment of Educational Progress). Atomistic tests are easier to use, cheaper, and probably more reliable; but holistic tests are potentially more valid, and in particular, Primary Trait Scoring is potentially more informative.

33

Atomistic Methods

The range of atomistic tests in common use illustrates their value. Saying "I gotta use words when I talk to you" suggests that vocabulary is a measure of skill in writing. Vocabulary tests are used for so many kinds of estimates of human ability that we might not even think of them as tests of skill in discourse. To be sure, we use the results of vocabulary tests for placement in freshman English and for admission to college or even graduate school, thus demonstrating that we correlate vocabulary development with general skill in discourse. But one look at any academic journal—or worse, the manuscripts as they are submitted—is enough to dispel the idea that the size of the vocabulary is a valid measure. Although one must have a large vocabulary in order to discourse well on a variety of topics, it does not follow that a large vocabulary in itself is enough to ensure skill in discourse. The vocabulary test is, at best, a device for finding out whether a person might control merely one feature necessary for skill in writing.

Variations of vocabulary tests have been designed. NAEP has used one that counts the average number of letters per word used by essay writers, but the results can't be associated with the quality of the writing, probably because word length in itself has little to do with aptness of choice, and averages conceal the more important issue of range. Sophisticated literary critics have examined short texts in terms of the etymology of words chosen, the percentage of polysyllables, or the rankings of words on word frequency lists for writing. The counting, even when intellectually complicated, can be satisfyingly exact, but until such counts are related to skills in discourse, we will not have learned much about how to evaluate writing samples.

A common test used for college entrance and many English achievement or "exit" examinations is a test of conventional usage and manuscript mechanics. Recent discussion about its misuse has centered on its billing as a test of writing skill. It is, of course, a test of social conformity, of how well a person recognizes the language forms most commonly used by those in authority in America. The test undoubtedly sorts out the people who will succeed in college, but that does not make it a test of skills in discourse.

We are more familiar with the use of larger syntactical or rhetorical units for measuring maturity or clarity in discourse. On one hand, we measure sentence length and complexity, we search out "T-units" or kinds of embedding to indicate the growth of sophistication in expressing ideas. The units can be described quite rigorously—perhaps almost as precisely as one can define words—so the tests can be reliable over a period of time even though the complexity of description may require expert readers dealing with small samples. In a parallel but less rigorous way, readability formulae are used to describe technical and business prose in order to identify what might be hard to read. Sometimes features of vocabulary are counted in the formulae, but most of the issues are related to syntax and sentence length. Since these larger units depend upon organization and subordination—that is, emphasis—they are more plausible symptoms of skill in discourse. The quality of the sentence may seem to be independent of the kind of discourse (a moot proposition, in fact, but conclusions about the maturity of writers based on studies of syntax seem to make the assumption, as do conventional literary descriptions of style) so gathering samples of writing is relatively easy and the information obtained is fairly specific (number of words, number of dependent clauses, kinds of embedding, etc.). Just a modest extension of the act of checking subordination within a sentence leads to examining conjunctions and other words which suggest emphasis within a paragraph, and thus leads to assumptions about coherence in discourse. Unfortunately we lack normative data, and our existing observations—the "lore" of coherence—may not be appropriate in a new age of nonverbal electronic communication. Although most moderately educated people have learned to accept changes in the lexicon of English and most scholars have learned to accept changes of usage and syntax, we are not well informed about fashions or basic changes of rhetorical conventions. Perhaps such changes occur in gross ways and are therefore conscious enough to be viewed merely as stylistic strategies. Still, an analogy to developments in filmmaking might be suitably cautionary. A young person brought up on current techniques of cinematic transition—abrupt shifts of space, time, and point of view—thinks the elaborate explicitness of films in the 1930s is slow, or even "verbal." Even those of us brought up on films of the thirties suffer from nostalgia when we view the old elaborateness. Similarly, because of our deep commitment to written language, especially to classic texts, we may have a much more difficult time responding to changes in rhetorical customs in prose. Research in such problems will always follow the fact of change, and the problem affects all of our examinations of discourse.

Some more complex atomistic observations appear to deal with elements of rhetoric and thus seem less atomistic. Rating scales seem to apply to the whole discourse. Papers which are scored in terms of organization, evidence, diction, or combinations of these or other rhetorical features may be nominally judged *in toto*; the named "features" are elements of discourse, but these features, in fact, are isolated from the context by a reader and scored separately—an atomistic system tied to abstract categories associated with traditional rhetorics. Often the definitions of categories are quite vague, and at best they may be arbitrary. After all, exactly what is *diction*? The scoring weight of a particular category is usually expressed in a fixed point system which is not adjusted for different kinds of discourse; there is no effort to adjust the points to tell, for example, whether evidence is as important in self-expression as in persuasion. And since organizational patterns may differ widely for different kinds of discourse—or for different subjects treated similarly—the precision of categories is more apparent than real. Various kinds of scoring guides, once popular and still represented in marking guides of freshman handbooks and on various diagnostic tests, are not reliable or even especially valid as ways of recording information about large samples of writing. They serve best as convenient shorthand for explaining judgments about writing to students.

Atomistic tests, then, may deal with the smallest units of discourse (vocabulary, usage, syntax), the kind which can be easily adapted to machine grading, or with relatively pervasive elements of discourse (concreteness, coherence, liveliness), which must be described by trained human readers. A user of the tests presumes that the correlation between mastery of the feature and the arts of discourse is close enough to permit practical judgments about skill in writing. NAEP gives the results of several of these kinds of examinations in its reports in *Writing Mechanics*. Even though they may not be valid and persuasive tests of discourse, they provide knowledge about particular features of language which are important to many of us. We often teach in terms of the specifics, and certainly our ability to talk about writing depends on the existence of reliably defined features and categories. We need more data about how features of writing relate to writing performance in the real world before we can be confident of our assumptions in the test world.

Holistic Methods

Holistic tests are based on the idea that a valid test of discourse depends upon the examination of a sample of discourse as a whole, not merely as a collection of parts. One need not assume that the whole is more than the sum of the parts—although I do—for it may be simply that the categorizable parts are too numerous and too complexly related to permit a valid report. Some recent efforts to combine human judgment with a computer's memory, at least at the pragmatic level, are based on this less demanding assumption.

If one decides that a valid (or publicly acceptable and persuasive) test requires both a sample of discourse and a human reaction, then one must elect some holistic system, precisely defining the segment of discourse to be evaluated. The writing sample must reflect the writer's choices rather than the testmaker's choices; the critical response must be affective as well as cognitive, and must interpret unconventional and creative language as well as report conventional devices. For purposes such as classroom placement or equivalency credit, where there are other procedures to assess individual exceptions, the ETS method and its variants are probably adequate and relatively simple. See Paul Diederich's most readable comments in *Measuring Growth in English* for a general review, and see his bibliography for leads to more technical accounts.

The methods perfected by ETS assume that excellence in one sample of one mode of writing predicts excellence in other modes—that is, good writing is good writing. Some allowance is made for "having a bad day" or other problems of the test situation. In contrast, the Primary Trait System developed under the auspices of NAEP[1] assumes that the writer of a good technical report may not be able to produce an excellent persuasive letter to a city council. A precise description on census of writing skills is far richer in information if the observations are categorized according to the purpose of the prose. The goal of Primary Trait Scoring is to define precisely what segment of discourse will be evaluated (e.g., presenting rational persuasion between social equals in a formal situation), and to train readers to render holistic judgments accordingly.

The chief steps in using the Primary Trait Scoring System are to define the universe of discourse, to devise exercises which sample that universe precisely, to ensure cooperation of the writers, to devise workable scoring guides, and to use the guides.

Choosing a Discourse Model

In order to report precisely how people manage different types of discourse, one must have a model of discourse which permits the identification of limited types of discourse and the creation of exercises which stimulate writing in the appropriate range but not beyond it. The three-part model Klaus and I selected was based on the purpose (goal, aim) of the discourse and reflected whether the character of the writing grew out of a focus on the writer, the audience, or the subject matter. (Perhaps we show the influence of Aristotle and his interpreters, and we will take any credit

---

[1] NAEP supported a scoring conference which included five people from NCTE: Robert Gorrell, William Irmscher, Richard Lloyd-Jones, Louis Milic, and Donald Seybold as well as Ellis Page, William Coffman and several staff test specialists. Later NAEP asked Carl H. Klaus and Lloyd-Jones to elaborate the system both in theory and with practical scoring guides. In developing the guides they were joined by Seybold and six others. The guides were then checked for feasibility by Westinghouse Learning Corporation under the direction of Louise Diana, who contributed substantially to the refining of the ideas.

we can earn by that allusion.) Contrasting available two- or four-part models may suggest the issues at stake and thus define our choice. We did not seriously consider more elaborate models, for example, Jakobson's six-part model.

If we had chosen a two-part model—say, Britton's notions of "specta-tor" and "participant" writing—we would have echoed the two main ob-jectives of the second round of NAEP's writing assessment: self-expression and social effectiveness. It is an excellent model for directing observations of the gradual socialization of children, but it tends to take for granted the demands of the subject, of information processing which is important to responsible adults and thus to the schools. The two-part division may be said to include some information processing as a part of a Kantian dis-covery of *a priori* forms within the self (temporal and spatial issues, for example), and on the other hand, to include some other information pro-cessing in the learning of standard public procedures for getting along in a society (report writing or business letter writing). Still, by limiting the observations about the writing to the participants in communication, the encoder and the decoder, the two-part division diminishes our sense of how the external reality influences our reasons for writing and how the code itself works.

If we had chosen a four-part model, such as the system elucidated fully by Kinneavy in *A Theory of Discourse*, we might have had a more exact-ing and theoretically satisfying system, but one that was unnecessarily complex for describing impromptu writing produced in 20- or 25-minute exercises. Kinneavy notes that the purposes of discourse may not only be self-centered, audience directed, and subject controlled, but they may be involved with manipulation of language for its own sake, as in literature. Given time, one may produce literary language in oratory, advertising, or graffiti, for example; playing with words may represent a pleasantly sub-versive motive which complicates any effort at writing, either enhancing or inhibiting its effectiveness in coping with other goals. Fond of language ourselves, Klaus and I hated to omit evidence of interest in the language in the code itself, but we also felt that the practical limits of our methods for getting samples of prose made extensive examination certainly mislead-ing. We therefore judged playfulness in language—manipulation of lan-guage forms for sheer pleasure—to be a part of self-expression. That is, we deliberately chose a model simpler than one we might have selected on purely theoretical grounds.

Perhaps, too, I should offer a practical caveat which is taken for granted by model builders: Motives are rarely pure. We write a single piece for many reasons; therefore, our practical judgments about the effectiveness of a particular sample of writing require the blending of the pure colors of the theoretical system into the earthier shades of actual performances. For example, I write to inform you about the system we devised, but I am not really trying to avoid persuading you of its usefulness, nor am I concealing the voices of the people who did the work and thus imposed their visions and conceptions on reality, nor do I refuse to play little games with the language. In short, the sharp categories of our discourse model probably must be blurred into continua, a kind of tri-polar surface upon which we might locate any particular rhetorical situation in order to schematize the blend of purposes implied, so we can then derive what must be the primary rhetorical traits and the particular verbal devices which should be associated with the trait.

Figure 1 depicts the model we actually chose. Explanatory, persuasive and expressive extremes are represented by the angles of the triangle. Each point is associated with the features of language ordinarily related to that goal of writing. For example, we view persuasive writing as audience oriented and therefore concerned with the appeals of classical rhetoric. Yet, we note that one of the traditional appeals is to logic, and certain persuasive situations tend toward the explanatory point of the triangle. Categorical organization and explicit evidence are important in such situations. Persuasion more dependent on ethical proof, on expressions of the character of the speaker, would be located more toward the expressive point of the triangle and would be more concerned with the devices suggesting the "voice" of the writer.

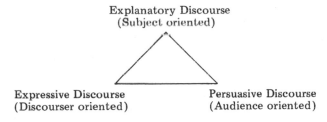

Explanatory Discourse
(Subject oriented)

Expressive Discourse   Persuasive Discourse
(Discourser oriented)   (Audience oriented)

Figure 1.

Figure 2 depicts a more complex model we rejected as more complicated than we could handle. Although the diagram suggests that transactional writing (perlocutionary) can usefully be divided into referential and persuasive writing, it also implies that illocutionary writing can blur the distinction between expressive and literary discourse. I have tried to suggest alternative terms without worrying about fine distinctions in order to imply how categories in the model represent tendencies in related models.

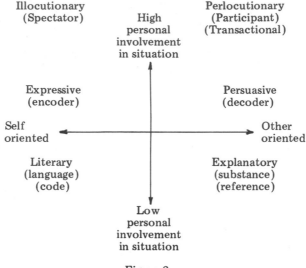

Figure 2.

Evaluation: The Real World and the World of Tests

The model categorizes discourse directly in terms of the purpose of discourses, so before trying to develop exercises for use in indirect testing, consider how we evaluate discourse directly. Exercises and scoring guides must eventually stand up as analogies for the direct experiences of writing.

In the real world, as opposed to the world of the testmaker, transactional discourse is judged by what it accomplishes. If one is trying to sell automobiles, the sales chart to some extent is a measure of the effectiveness of the discourse, although the facts of a malfunctioning vehicle or impoverished customers may cloud the issue. So too with all of the types of persuasion outlined by Aristotle; each can be judged by its effect, although each may be perverted by some exigency in the situation. When the transaction is explanatory, as a set of directions or in a textbook, the quality of the explanation may be judged by whether the reader is able to carry on the procedures as directed. Even the ability to carry on a discussion in which the understanding of an idea is necessary becomes a test of the explanation. Put simply, a transaction implies a response; if the reader makes the appropriate response, the writer has written well. Not all situations are equally demanding; selling a car to a bankrupt cyclist is more difficult than selling a drink to a wealthy alcoholic, but each can be judged by a practical outcome. In the test world, nothing really happens, so some method of analysis and description must be devised to replace the observation of the effect.

In the real world expressive discourse makes a writer feel better and know more—it is the language of discovery. To the extent that an audience is involved, expressiveness is shared language. We say that the author expresses our ideas. When James Kinneavy (1971) analyzes the Declaration of Independence as a piece of expression, which it primarily is, he reveals it to us as if it were our own expression, if we were clever enough to have thought it (pp. 409 ff.). That issue of expression for the collective mind is now confused by the fact that the nation honors the text without reading it; we might speculate that many people would oppose it, if they read it thoughtfully, for it asserts the value system of its authors and not of many current Americans. The same might be said for most revolutionary documents, love letters, and barroom chitchat. What happens is probably internal. Even if a revolution or a barroom brawl is generated, the expression is responsible only to the extent that it helped each participant find a form in language which enabled him or her to discover personal beliefs. These individuals were not persuaded; rather they found, borrowed, or stole a form for their own inchoate feelings. With some qualifications, as much can be said to define literature as the language of formation and discovery in symbols. Even in the real world it is difficult to judge expression. Each reader speaks for one person. Some especially sensitive literary critics or psychoanalytic observers can guide the judgments of most readers, but even literary scholars prefer to describe expressive pieces as social commentary that should be judged in a world of transactions. And since the aims of discourse are rarely unmixed, such evasions have merit. In the test world the difficulty of dealing with expressiveness has often led us to pretend that it doesn't exist.

Developing Exercises

Perhaps I have eased into the second step of using Primary Trait Scoring—devising exercises which in fact stimulate respondents to write as well as they can within the narrowly defined kind of discourse to be examined. For all holistic testing, any exercise must be within the legitimate range of knowledge of the writer. An exercise about farming penalizes city children, one about vacations favors the prosperous, and one about making complaints will vary in its power according to the writer's social class. A situation which will bore one child will threaten another and baffle still another. The results will reflect experience in situations as much as skill in manipulating language forms. A wide open subject, such as that allowed in conventional holistic scoring, permits each writer to find a personally satisfying way to respond, but in Primary Trait Scoring a stimulus must generate writing which is situation bound. The writer can't just do his or her own thing. The more one restricts the situation in order to define a purpose and stimulate performance of a particular kind, the greater the chances that the exercise will fall outside of respondents' experiences. The testmaker must deal with the problem directly.

Identifying the Kind of Discourse

First, we must isolate the type of discourse to be evoked. On a theoretical basis, we might want to sample all areas of the model triangle, and perhaps á person with a good command of theory and lots of practical experience in relating the features of discourse to situations would mark spots on the model and create exercises to fit. Partly because we inherited exercises from the first round of the NAEP's writing assessment and from preliminary work done on the second round, we located existing exercises on the model. We imagine that most teachers practiced in creating classroom exercises will also create the situation first. Then they can analyze the rhetorical implications, placing the exercise on the model; this will serve as an aid in discovering the features which characterize writing in the prescribed mode.

Suppose one begins with a typical classroom assignment: "Write a letter to the principal suggesting some improvement in our school." That seems to be a routinely persuasive situation roughly conforming to Aristotle's strictures about deliverative discourse. We might assume that a principal is a mature and responsible person who will respond rationally to a detailed, factual description of a condition which requires change, so much of the presentation will probably be referential discourse. A principal concerned about pupils' feelings might respond to evidence of expressiveness, but that would be a secondary consideration. We probably would locate the exercise fairly close to the line between explanatory and persuasive discourse, closer to the persuasive end. If parents were the audience, we might posit that a larger expressive dimension would be appropriate, and we might consider that the usefulness of wheedling would push the exercise closer to pure persuasion. The specifics of this example, as in almost any proposed exercise, are open to discussion, but the issue for the testmaker is to try to identify the possibilities through careful examination of the situation and any verbal cues in the assignment itself. So long as the assumptions are explicit, the user of the test can interpret the results fairly.

Trials

Preliminary trials of proposed exercises are essential to ensure that respondents will understand the situation as the designers intend. One does not expect a student writer to make a conscious analysis parallel to that of the designer, but the writer must understand the situation in such a way that discourse in the appropriate mode is generated. The writer's duty is to perform aptly, but the designer's task is to create a situation in which that apt performance will illustrate the writer's competence within a particular mode of discourse.

The trials reveal whether or not the expected kind of discourse is evoked, and as importantly they suggest what kind of cooperation the exercise encourages. If an exercise happens to evoke consistently a kind of writing which the designers did not expect, they may simply recategorize the exercise to conform with what has happened, although they should attempt to rationalize the change. When we found that a hypothetically persuasive exercise about women's place in society provoked mostly statements of feelings about women's place, we tinkered a little with the phrasing and thus created an expressive exercise with an appropriate scoring guide (see pp. 60-66). We might also have changed the exercise drastically to require arguments about the Equal Rights Amendment—a more clearly persuasive situation—but that would have required our respondents to have special knowledge and probably would have distorted excessively our view of the quality of the writing as such.

Motivation

One can never wholly separate the quality of the writing from the knowledge of the subject and probably should not try. Yet, if one is to learn about a national sample of several age groups, and if by law one cannot identify individuals or school districts, then one has to get the cooperation of the writers without the implicit threats of bad grades or angry school boards. Part of that cooperation must come from giving the writer a satisfying task. Knowledge of the subject is part of the satisfaction. The objections made about lack of motivation in writing for the first round of NAEP's writing assessment may have to be doubled for the second because Primary Trait Scoring enforces restrictions which may make the tasks less attractive.

Still, some illustrative observations about how the exercises affect motivation can be suggested. The more the stimulus includes material intended to suggest prewriting instructions given in textbooks, the greater the confusion. Each prewriting question provokes its own answer. In fact, each addition to the stimulus produces a possible distraction, and distractions seem to lessen the attractiveness of the task. Certain images create trouble. "Bananas," for example, seems to provoke pornographic or scatological responses. Bill collectors seem to be exceedingly threatening to some people. When we tried an explanatory-persuasive exercise to evoke a serious letter to correct an error in computer billing, we got a number of amusing responses, but when we tried to revise the exercise to encourage humorous literary-expressive responses by making the situation more absurd, we found that the increase in the number who could joke about computers and over-due bills was small and, strangely, the number which dealt effectively with the problem in serious, highly conventional terms became larger. In both versions a substantial number of respondents were merely hostile.

In general, expressive exercises seemed to draw more enthusiastic responses than did transactional ones, probably because writing expressively is to some extent its own reward. Make-believe transactions present a mild contradiction of terms and that may tempt one to underestimate the skills in handling practical situations. Especially for nine-year-olds writing seems to be fun, but older students more often seem to view writing as a chore. Probably no simple answer to motivation can be offered for all test situations, but it should be a concern, and perhaps it would be wise to have uninvolved observers read papers and comment on the seriousness with which writers approach their tasks. In short, finding likely topics within the range of all the respondents and challenging enough to promote serious efforts despite the lack of any "payoff" remains a problem. And a 55-minute test period is still only 55 minutes, so tests are limited to extemporaneous production. That does not demonstrate what a serious person might be able to do in occasions which permit time for reconsideration and revision. Editing allowed in a 55-minute period should not be considered revision.

Scoring Guides

The practical problems of devising suitable exercises would fill a handbook of operational lore, but creating intelligible scoring guides without violating the chaste theoretical model requires patient labor, frequent trial readings, and substantial theoretical background—on the average, sixty to eighty hours of professional time per exercise, not counting the time required to administer the proposed exercise to get samples, nor the time required to try out the proposed guide. Once the guide is created for a particular exercise—and the guides are specific for each situation—then presumably any bright and verbal person can use it.

A scoring guide consists of (1) the exercise itself, (2) a statement of the primary rhetorical trait of the writing which should be elicited by the exercise (a kind of statement of the limited test objective), (3) an interpretation of the exercise indicating how each element of the stimulus is presumed to affect the respondent (a kind of hypothesis about performance), (4) an interpretation of how the situation of the exercise is related to the posited primary trait (a synthesis of #2 and #3), (5) a system for defining the shorthand which is to be used in reporting descriptions of the writing (the actual scoring guide), (6) samples of papers which have been scored (definition of the score points), and (7) discussions of why each sample paper was scored as it was (extensions of the definitions).

Most of the guides of persuasive or referential writing use numbers (scores) which indicate a value placed on the observed performances. Usually 4 or 5 is a highly competent performance, 1 is a serious but quite inadequate response; other symbols are used to indicate a failure to engage the exercise. Since score points are defined in detailed discussions, the usual arguments about using even or odd numbers of scoring categories do not apply. The middle number is not necessarily an "average" performance. Excellent prose which is an inappropriate response to a situation may well be rated 1, in some writing situations a top score might appropriately be awarded to prose judged to be nonstandard dialect. Expressive prose often was described in terms of the kinds of response made—not presuming, for example, that either categorical or associative organizational systems were to be preferred, or even that lots of concrete detail was self-evidently better than well-knit abstractions. Simply, the score points indicated what the writer did. Each score point is described in detail in terms of what language features might be expected.

Perhaps in an ideal world of brilliant rhetoricians one would know in advance the features which would define a 2 or a 4 paper, but we took papers gathered in trial runs, examined them carefully to see what features actually were chosen to solve the rhetorical problem, and then wrote the descriptions to conform with the expectations established by the sample. Usually, we found many quite legitimate solutions which we had not imagined. We were delighted by the inventiveness of respondents and quickly learned that even highly structured situations permit a variety of appropriate responses.

Guides for some of the released exercises have been published by NAEP; one example is appended to this chapter. Anyone who wishes to use this method should undoubtedly read over several guides before devising new ones. Each guide was constructed by three people, one acting as secretary for the group. Then it was given a feasibility check by an independent observer who used the guides to train readers. They, in turn, rated papers obtained in the original trials and previously rated by those who devised the guides. The reliability was judged to be at least as good as that obtained in more conventional holistic scoring, although those data, too, are better presented by the people who worked on them for NAEP. Writing Report 05-W-02 ("Expressive Writing") provides an extended discussion of the scoring of three exercises.

When to Use Primary Traits

The questions about whether to use the method concern the convenience of development and administration, the validity, and the amount of information obtained. In terms of convenience for the tester, Primary Trait Scoring is more difficult than other methods. One hopes that the evident need for extreme care forces the testmaker to develop a better instrument, but that argument, I am aware, tastes like sweet lemons.

For validity most tests of writing depend heavily on face values. Our usual decision about whether a given sample of writing is to be judged as good, apart from situations of actual use, depends on the opinion of qualified reviewers. If enough reviewers of various biases accept a piece of writing as good—especially if the reviewers live in widely separated places over a period of time—then the writing is accepted. Such judgments are not much help to a person who needs a quick report on a large number of small samples. As a result, the ETS method of searching out "qualified" judges and calibrating their reactions to a single reporting code is a reasonable compromise. To be sure, the validity of the judgment is limited by the ability of the judges, and even under carefully planned scoring conditions, the judges rate in gross terms. At times one has the sense that a household yardstick is being used to measure the diameter of a cylinder in an automobile engine. To ensure high reliability, one must accept very broad ranges. Various atomistic tests may be correlated to such holistic judgments and thus acquire the same face validity, although necessarily there is some loss of value in the transfer. Atomistic tests can also be correlated to other outcomes, such as success in college, but this does not really provide a valid statement about skill in discourse. Primary Trait Scoring also depends to some extent on the face authority of the readers, but even more on the competence of the people who make the exercises and the guides. A user of the test can easily examine just what the testers thought they were examining. The test thus gains credibility in its openness. Not the authority of the reader but the persuasiveness of the scoring guide becomes the issue.

The final advantage of the Primary Trait method is the amount of information which can be taken from a piece of writing. To some extent one must know less to know more. A sharper focus eliminates some of the penumbra of a general skill, but it gives a sharper view of the complex of particular skills required to do a given task, and therefore increases the likelihood that we will be able to identify strengths and weaknesses precisely. If we find that our respondents, in trying to persuade responsible authority, do not provide clear objectives, evident transitions, and apt evidence, and if at the same time we find that our respondents are able to present vividly concrete narratives from a first person point of view with implied transitions (or stop-action associative connections), then we can begin to make far more useful comments about their skills in writing. Granted, we still need much stylistic study of exactly what features of language are necessary in different situations, and until we have such work we will probably have to create questionable make-do scoring guides based on describing trial runs of exercises. Still, unless we focus on one type of discourse at a time, we will be limited to a vague global view of the moon. The Primary Trait method doesn't offer an immediate shuttle rocket to descriptions of writing, but it does suggest a research tool which might permit more persuasive conclusions than we have yet been able to reach.

APPENDIX

To suggest the process of evolving adequate Primary Trait Scoring guides we are appending scoring guides for two writing tasks. For one of the tasks (Children on Boat essay), we are including an early draft of a scoring guide and the revised, final form. For the other task (Woman's Place essay), we are simply including the final scoring guide. Both guides together illustrate the possibilities of Primary Trait analysis and scoring.

Writing Task: Children on Boat

Respondents were given a printed photograph of five children playing on an overturned rowboat. The picture is copied in NAEP report 05-W-02, "Expressive Writing," along with additional reports of the scoring of the exercise itself. The task was presented to a sample of ages 9, 13, and 17 in 1974. The actual task and the original draft of the scoring guide are reproduced here. The final scoring guide given to raters follows that. These guides do not appear in the report.

Directions: Look carefully at the picture. These kids are having fun jumping on the overturned boat. Imagine you are one of the children in the picture. Or if you wish, imagine that you are someone standing nearby watching the children. Tell what is going on as he or she would tell it. Write as if you were telling this to a good friend, in a way that expresses strong feelings. Help your friend FEEL the experience too. Space is provided on the next three pages.

NAEP Scoring Guide: Children on Boat

Background

Primary Trait. Imaginative Expression of Feeling through Inventive Elaboration of a *Point of View.*

Rationale. The test is whether a writer can project him/herself into a situation, find a role and an appropriate audience, and then reveal an attitude toward the material in relation to the role—a complex writing task. The picture is full of information; as in life, there is more information than a writer can use; the writer must *choose* appropriate facets of the situation consistently to serve a *purpose*. As in any photograph, time is arrested, so to explain what is going on, a writer must *invent* circumstances consistent with what is given. Weak writers will be tempted to explain the details separately, if at all; perhaps because a weak writer cannot really get into the situation, he or she gets no sense of the whole. A strong, well-elaborated point of view will relate and control the events.

Note the important features of the instructions. "Look carefully at the picture." The writer is expected to study the facts, to perceive detail, but if he or she has trouble getting going, the observation that the kids are having fun jumping on an overturned boat will help.

Then the writer is given one of two roles—that of a child in the picture or that of a person nearby. The latter may be child or adult. It is also possible to have either role filled by a person writing much later in reminiscent response to the picture, but the writer is still expected to maintain a personal relationship to the events of the picture.

Finally are the three verbs of crucial instruction, "Tell," "Write," and "Help." "Tell" suggests an oral manner, although it probably does not require it, but "as he or she would tell it" provides additional pressure to be natural. In fact, it encourages role playing, a strong "I" voice, and that can cause some difficulty in reading papers by mature writers who are trying to imitate children. Probably those who attempt extremely difficult point of view problems should be read leniently, because they are demonstrating notable competence. The second verb introduces the "good friend," an instruction that may encourage dialogue but implies that a crucial element of strongly realized point of view is an audience to which one directs a tone. This too may invite private jokes, and sometimes the overt concessions to audience may be missing, yet "I" requires "thou" so the issue may be very important. The issue of feeling finishes the second verb and occupies the third (which also makes another reference to audience) so one expects a governing emotion to unify the paper—the "I" is defined at least in part by attitude (feeling) toward the materials of the picture. The selection and ordering of detail, and the invention of self, tone, and attitude should make the best papers highly structured. So much control in 20 minutes is outstanding, so we judge that even a paper which maintains good technical control and order with closure is still excellent.

Original Scoring Guide

Rubric.

Non-rateable. *Does not refer to the picture at all.*
The paper could have been written by someone who had not even seen the picture. Any paper that refers either to five children or to an overturned rowboat (or to both), no matter how minimally, must be assumed to have been stimulated by the picture; therefore it is rateable. Any paper that does not refer to either of those elements must be scored as non-rateable because it then invents its own problems and is irrelevant to the categories of this rubric.

1. *There is no real entry into the imaginary world of the picture even though there is enough descriptive information to prove the writer tried to address the issue.*
Technically, most of these papers are incoherent; that is, the information does not stick together or drive to a particular point. Details or bits of information may be named, but do not fit into a situation; lists of observations do not reveal a perspective. There may be relatively few lapses in temporal or spatial point of view because the writer attempts so little, although it also is true that notable confusion of technical point of view justifies a "1." Some papers may be quite long, but they represent mere description of the picture, repetition, or irrelevant speculation. Others may be too brief to create a world. The writer may possibly name a reader, as suggested in the instruction, but no definition of information seems to result. Some merely remain as observers of a photograph.

2. *The writer accepts the world of the picture and thus has an appropriate and identifiable point of view, but is unable to create any structure to his/her presentation of that world.* The opposite of this can also be true. That is, the writer has created structure but his/her point of view is either inconsistent or flawed in other ways, such as temporal or spatial.
The data in "2" papers may permit the reader to construct an organizational pattern consistent with the point of view, but the writer leaves the pattern to be inferred. There are relatively few internal transitions expressed. Attitude may be stated but not illustrated; narratives may be suggested but not worked out; theses may or may not be stated, but they don't control much; in short, the writer enters the world of the picture, but is not sure where he or she is. As a result the writer may cite details which don't actually contradict but don't really harmonize— clusters of perhaps-related notions that don't make a whole. He or she may invent incidents outside of the picture without relating them to items in the picture. Often there are errors in technical point of view—tense sequence, for example—but these are symptoms of the failure to reveal the writer's place in relation to correct sequences in nonstandard dialects of English. Issues relating to dialect are not part of this rating, so scorers should be cautious in reporting as failures what might be alternative forms.

3. *These papers are generally competent in creating a realized point of view toward the world of the picture.*

The temporal and spatial point of view is controlled, expressed in strong leads or topic sentences or transitions, but the development is uneven. Elaboration is flawed, and the attitude may be merely named instead of presented to "help your friend feel," perhaps because details are inadequate, excessive, or unclear.

Narratives, if used, are sketched in (more than suggested) but still are left with gaps or other unevenness. Theses or attitudes may be named, and somewhat supported, but do not govern the whole paper. Excess details, if they occur, are a flaw when they don't in fact aid the pattern, even if they don't obscure it. Some patterns, however, encourage invention well beyond what is actually in the picture.

Note: The scoring of categories 1, 2, and 3 must be done on a main thrust basis. That is, the paper that contains mere description of the "1" category can become a "2" paper later on in it. That is to say that some writers write papers that move from one category to another—they are not neatly written in just one category (some essentially "2" papers can contain a whole section that moves it into "3" category). Therefore if the paper is mainly a "1" ("2" or "3") with some elements of another category, the paper should be scored on what the writer has mainly done. This consideration does not arise in the "4" or "5" categories because "4" and "5" papers must be structurally whole.

4. *Temporal and spatial point of view sustained by consistent narrative or attitude, developed by evocative detail, representing a strongly felt perspective.*

These papers are neat—loose ends have been tied up or cut off. The writer's role is evident; he or she probably is able to create the role without even making an explicit issue of the relation to the audience, but at the same time shows concern for his or her attitudes and ideas in concrete terms. The papers often have closure, although a strong paper without closure can still be rated in this category.

5. *These papers have all the neatness of a "4" and shape the facts of the situation into a highly structured, intelligent statement. The statement can be positive or negative and can be accomplished through controlled as well as through explicit interpretation.*

These unusually mature papers represent a perspective that fuses emotion and intellect into a single statement. If narrative order is chosen, the story will suggest meanings beyond the events themselves—not as a tacked-on sentiment, but as integral development. An essay will show a strong interpretative intelligence. These papers are likely to present ideas implicitly rather than explicitly.

Notes: "3" is not the midpoint of a five-point scale; in this rating "5" is exceptionally good. "1" and "2" represent failures to realize point of view; "3" and "4" represent degrees of success. "5" is a rarity of success mostly to be found among 17 year olds and adults.

Strategies and Devices. Although point of view is the trait being examined, this trait can be perceived only in reference to the information presented; therefore, especially in good papers, a rater may seem to be judging the quality of the detail. Such quality is determined by how well it extends and confirms the personality and perspective of the writer. The imagination is required in order to conceive of the perspective and to select and invent details from the picture and its implied antecedents so that a feeling is expressed. The object of the secondary descriptions for this item is to identify the strategies by which the point of view is made to operate. Although particular choices are not necessarily better than others, some devices allow the writer more options and therefore more complexity in expressing an idea and more fullness in realizing a situation.

First identify the speaker as one of the five children shown in the picture or as an observer. We will count an adult recalling participation as one of the children as a child speaker; the distinctions can be recorded in the next item. The issue is that the writer records his or her experiences directly. We can hypothesize that speakers dealing with their own experiences will be more precise in controlling point of view. Mark 1, 2, or 0.

1. *Point of view of one of the five children.* This also includes papers in which the writer says, "If I were one of the five children." In these papers the writer is not clearly one of the children but he/she is attempting to take that point of view.

2. *Point of view of the observer.* This category also includes papers in which it is difficult to tell which point of view is being taken.

0. *Both of the above.* These are essentially papers in which the writer has misunderstood the directions to take either the point of view of the children or of the observer. Usually these papers are two separate essays—one in which the writer has assumed a child's point of view, and one assuming an observer's.

Note: When an observer joins the children in the play, the point of view is still "2" because the observer makes a "6th" person playing and therefore is not one of the original five.

Describing the events as they occur is more likely to result in immediacy, although it also may introduce various kinds of complications in transition and development. Mark either 3, TH, or 4.

3. *Viewed from present.* If the point of view wavers in time or creates a present frame for past events, then "3" should be marked. If the present tense controls a part of the paper, we can assume a desire to create immediacy. Mere absence of the past tense market(-ed) is not, in all dialects of American English, evidence of present tense, so readers should be careful to observe adverbs as well as affixes.

TH. *This category is for "time:hypothetical" papers.* These are papers that are written entirely in the "If I were on the boat," or, "If I were an observer I would do—." These papers often include future references such as "When I get on the boat I will do—." It should be stressed that this category is reserved for papers that never leave the hypothetical, as many papers contain some hypothetical structures but then settle on either the present or the past. Therefore any paper that contains something other than hypothetical structures should be scored in the appropriate other category.

4. *Viewed as events in the past.*

Some writers will choose a framing strategy for some or almost all the explanations. Basically this strategy calls for a doubled perspective on the events so the writer can develop an idea by implicit contrasts. Most of the writers will be other than one of the five children, and the frame will create their role. However, merely creating an outside self is not enough; the writer must use the contrast between his or her perspective and that of the children on the boat. Since we hypothesize that the simplest development would use a single perspective, that is, anyone who has established a double point of view must also have established a single point—we suggest merely a "present-not present" marking of whether a frame exists. By definition, papers scored in primary scoring cannot create a successful frame, although possibly a writer may be scored 1 because he has attempted a frame and simply confused the issue.

5. *Uses, at least in part, a framing strategy for the point of view.*

Another device of distancing the observer from the events is to create a fantasy. Most papers will probably deal with reporting the events and providing logical interpretations of what is going on. They might even try to create a sense of the pleasure of games (e.g., king of the hill) but the papers remain in the literal world.

Some writers will try to reproduce the game fantasies of the children on the boat. Probably the most interesting ones will be wholly set in a world of pirates or shipwrecks in the child's mind, but others will use the frame to permit entry into the world of fantasy. This should be scored as "present-not present." Merely positing the fantasy is not enough. There must be at least a bare minimum of elaboration which allows the reader to enter the writer's fantasy.

6. *Uses fantasy as a device of extending the perspective.*

Another way to reveal multiple perspective is in the use of dialogue. Although casting the explanation as a drama would be the most extreme form of realizing multiple perspective, even trace uses of a dialogue indicate an awareness of different stances, so on a "present-not present" basis scorers should report the use of a dialogue within the answer. Quotation marks are not essential; the clarity of audience awareness is. This is to say that a statement must be clearly intended as an oral statement for a listener, real or imagined. The statement cannot be speculation or any other remark that could simply be made to one's self aloud.

7. *Dialogue is used.*

Final Scoring Guide

ENTIRE EXERCISE

0   No response, sentence fragment
1   Scorable
2   Illegible or illiterate
3   Does not refer to the picture at all
9   I don't know

USE OF DIALOGUE

0   Does not use dialogue in the story.
1   Direct quote from one person in the story. The one person may talk more than once. When in doubt whether two statements are made by the same person or different people, code 1. A direct quote of a thought also counts. Can be in hypothetical tense.
2   Direct quote from two or more persons in the story.

POINT OF VIEW

0   Point of view cannot be determined, or does not control point of view.
1   Point of view is consistently one of the five children. Include "If I were one

of the children. . . " and recalling participation as one of the children.

2   Point of view is consistently one of an observer. When an observer joins the children in the play, the point of view is still "2" because the observer makes a sixth person playing. Include papers with minimal evidence even when difficult to tell which point of view is being taken.

TENSE

0   Cannot determine time, or does not control tense. (One wrong tense places the paper in this category, except drowned in the present.)

1   Present tense—past tense may also be present if not part of the "main line" of the story.

2   Past tense—If a past tense description is acceptable brought up to present, code as "past." Sometimes the present is used to create a frame for past events. Code this as past, since the actual description is in the past.

3   Hypothetical time—Papers written entirely in the "If I were on the boat" or "If I were there, I would." These papers often include future references such as "when I get on the boat 1 will." If part is hypothetical and rest past or present and tense is controlled, code present or past. If the introduction, up to two sentences, is only part in past or present then code hypothetical.

Sample Responses.

Categories

Age	Dialogue	Point of View	Tense
	0	0	0

13   Well we are playing a game of monsters the boy is trying to swim away but the monster grabed him by the arm. The other boy is trying to get around the other monster and the monster is ready to grab him. The other girl sitting is drowning and gasbin for air.

17   The children are really having a fun time They are throwing it looks like little stones into the water. All of us were laughing and have a great time. A friend and another friend got on each side of the boat and started to jump up and down. All the other ones got really excited and started yelling. The blond hair kid almost fell in when the boat started to rock. All of us laughed. We all had so much fun we were trying to keep our balance but it was really hard. The boat was rocking so hard that all of us practically fall in. I think most of them were relations. They never had so much fun and were fascinated by the the sights and boats we were the only ones there at the time which made it good be cause we could laugh and joke more we really had a fun day. I wish we could do that again Ths time, I want you to come along. We haven't had this much fun in a long time.

	0	0	1

13   Look at the children jumping on the boat. They're balancing on the overturned boat. How looks like fun! We could make it a sliding board and everyone can play. or tilt it and make a see saw out of it. Maybe if we could turn it over we could put it in the water and go out into the lake, river, whatever it is. Someone could be a captain and the others can be passengers. Let's do it!

0   1   0

13   I was having such a great time. It was as though I was doing something that
no other kid was able to. As though I was older than 5 or 6. You should try this
sometimes. Its like playing house and being the mother of all those little kids.
Even though we all are the same age. When playing some of the kids play like
their younger than me. Thats what I mean mostly by my experience. on the
boat. I hope you can come and play on the boat with me tomorrow. I know
you would enjoy this as much as Mike, Cindy and the other kids did. It was
really great. You can even pretend to be sliding down a great big rock. You
can come and create with us.

17   Wow! We had the best time down at the park today. Ricky Cindy Jimmy
and I went *exploring*. We pretended to be Pirates who were stranded on a
deserted Island. All of us were trying to find a way to escape from the Island.
Then Captain Jimmy found a capsized boat on a derserted beach, at least we
thought it was deserted. But ther a gang of enemy pirates came and attacked
us from all sides, but we held them back and used the boat as a shelter against
their swords and Guns. Of course in the end we won the fight. We were all
overjoyed at the victory We jumped up and down and all around. Then we
were faced with the problem of getting off the Island once more. but we
weren't dummies we knew the other pirates must have had a boat! So we look
all day long till we found the enemies big ship. Onward for home we all
chimed in and we headed across the long wide ocean for home.
    But that was all right by me because I was hungry for lunch and I didn't
want to miss the cartoons at 12:30!!

0   1   1

17   Jumping and running on the boat is very enjoyable. Up we jump and down
we float. I feel as if I could sail the boat around the world and back. The salty
sea air blows through my nostrils. My body feels engulfed in this exotic salt
concoction The wind beats against my cheeks
    The white, glistening, enamel underside of the boat feels like silk to the
touch. The trees are alive, pulsating watching our childish games.
    I feel like I could play forever. No concept of time, no responsibilities, no
stresses encourage my exuberance.
    My body has separated from my spirit. I am no longer encaged in a prison
of bones and skin. These are no barriers now. I can do whatever I want,
whenever I want to do it.

0   1   2

13   Cindy, youll never believe what happened yesterday! Four kids and I went to
a dock and we turned over a boat. all of us got on it and we were trying to
kept our balience on it. after a while one boy sat down and started shaking the
whole boat. We tried to keep our palience. We all managed it.

17   Yesterday when we were at the lake we had a grand time. Steve Lori, Sue,
Jody and I had the whole day to paly. It was a chilly day so we didn't want to
get in the water or fall in. While going for a walk, we found at someone elses
at cabin on the dock an overturned boat. We jumped and played king of the
boat whiling we were struggling to keep from being pushed in. This was
difficult because as we moved the boat would rock from side to side. It was a

tieter toter rolling log. King of the mountian gone. Stevie won. becauce he was the only boy.

But he got in lots of trouble because he pushed Sue in. Even if he did win, winning isn't rewarding when he had to end our fun in such a way.

0   1   3

9   I would tip the Boat over and push it in the water. And then
I would go for a Ride.
I would jump in the water.
I would Push it in the water while evey Body.
I would push evey Body off the Boat.

0   2   0

9   Well, five children are standing on an over-turned boat. All of them are having fun jumping and hopping on it. It was a pretty windy day and the girl could have fallen in the lake. I thought one of them was going to hurt themselves by jumping and sprane their ankle. Three boats are tied to a booy in the lake.

13   Me and some of the kids were at the lake the other day. We saw some little kids playing on an overturned boat. Some were falling and slipping and sliding. It was fun to watch them. They acted like clowns. There were six boats and a house behind some trees in the background. On the other side were houses between some trees. There were two girls and three boys. The girls were wearing coats. one had a bonnet on. the other had short pants. But the other had long pants. The boys all had coats on.

17   This happen yesterday, their we five kid on a boat. they were all having alot of fun and if you were there you probaly you play with them. Like they were jumping up and down and make believe they were sailing it upside down. They were like jumping off and on. It was very great to be so small and do the same thing there did.

0   2   1

9   The children are on top of the boat walking around. They are trying to balance themselfs so they won't fall. One of them is balancing sitting down on the boat.

13   Look at those people on that boat. One is acting like he is on a horse. The little boy is jumping up and down. One girl bending over, the geggest girl is watching the other girl who is bending over. The other boy is also bending over. It senes like they are acting like they are on a boat in a storm on the sea. One the side of the lake.

17   the kid are haveing fun playing on the boat. trying to see who can walk on the boat without falling. The child siteing down is rocking the boat to make it even harder.

0   2   2

9   There were five children as I see, and they were all jumping on an over turned boat. I was standing about 50 feet away. They were all having so much fun. One was kneeling, one was jumping, one was running, one was standing still and one was blancing herself from falling in the water. I wish so much that I

was there to. Because they were having all so much fun, and I love jumping on boats.

13   These five kids were jumping on this overturned boat. Well I was just standing there watching them, when this little girl fell off and hurt herself. It was not bad. When the kids have left the boat I went over to the boat and looked at it. It had wholes and dents in it like I have never seen. I carried the boat to this boat fixer and he tried to fix it. Then he told me to try it out. So I put it on the water, got in it, and started drifting. Then sudenly it sunk with me. I got it out then looked at it and I seen it had a whole in it. I took it back to the boat fixer and the patched the whole up. Then I went back to the dock and tried it out and it worked good. The next day the same kids had turned the boat over and started it. I was disscused

17   I saw these kids on a boat one day and I mean they were really freaking out on this overturned boat. I mean they were having the time of their lives on this thing. I really don't know what they saw in it but it looked like fun. So I kicked them off and played on it by myself for 3 hours. Then they came back and kicked me off. So then I just watched. They were hopping up and down on this thing. I couldn't be how much fun they were having on it. I mean I was there for 3 hours and had the worst time of my life on the stupid boat.

                          0   2   3
9   I would feel very sad because I couldn't play. I would also feel lonley because I wouldn't have any one to play with.
I would wish I had someone to play with me.
I would ask my mom if I coult play and she would say yes and I would be happy and when I asked my friends if I could stay they would say yes and I would feel even happier.

                          1   1   0
9   One day we was at the shore. I and Jim, Chip, Brad, and Bill We was play on an over turned boat and we was pretending that we was pirates on an stormy sea and was ship wreck and the life boat tipped over and we was waving for help. When we got back on shore we told everyone what happened there then we pretend we was on an little island on the coast of Mexico and the little boat was the island We was waving for help, But we had to spend the night there just like I figured. I told them we shouldn't have gone that far and I said I knew it—I knew it!! And so when got back finnally we was not glad we wanted to pretend to visit another island like that so we pretended that we were stranded on another island and we were pretending that the over turned boat was the island again this was a far off island anmed Parkerson we like that island very much. even better than the other one we pretended at was better we had lots more fun.

13   Boy, today I had fun with my friends today. We were playing by the lake on a boat that was turned upside down. Christie almost fell into the water because the boat got a little wet. I just managed to grab her by the coat! I didn't know it but I stepped into the wet spot and I slipped too. Gaye managed to grab ME by the collar of my coat and she practically chocked me to death. But she still got me up. It was a pretty funny scene because while she was pulling me up I was hauling up Christie.

After the excitement died down us kids were pretending to be pirates. We couldn't play it very good the boat was turned upside down but we managed.

Little Johnny wanted to be the captain so we had to let him or else he would have cried, and I don't like that! Before we started playing pirates I had to take Christie home so she could get some slacks on because she had on only short and her leg were so cold they were turning red. With that water as cold as it was Christie was lucky she didn't fall into the water.

I'm glad the guys waited for me and Christie because I was the pretty little lady that gets captured by the pirates, and they are going to make me walk the *plank*! But I'm not really going to jump into the water. I thought Little Johnny was a great chaptain but I'm sorry we had to stop playing because our mothers called us to come in and have supper. We'll probably play pirates tomorrow and I hope to be the pretty lady again. The End

	1	1	1

13 If I was jumping on a boat. I would tell my freind. It is very fun jumping up and down on the boat. Sometimes when you jump hard enough it take your stomach. You can slide on the boat. You can play games on the boat. You can have on slick shoes you can't hardly stand up. If I were one I would take off my coat and put it down on the boat and let us take turns pulling each and other on it. Or I might just get a pair of skates and skate on it. You ort to try it. It is fun when you have some of freinds with so there can be more fun. It is more fun with freinds than by yourself.

	1	1	2

9 There were four other children besides me. We were all jumping on a turned over boat. I fell in the lake. The water was shallow. The other kids started laughing at me so I pushed them in. When they came out I laughed at them and I said I got you back. Then we all started laughing. We started watching the boats. We had a contest on who could jump the most and then jump into the lake the farthest.

17 Yesterday Pauls Dad bought a NEW boat. He took it down to his cabin on Lake Chelan and took us boating, we asked if we could take it out on the water alone. Paul's Dad *said no*, then he pulled it ashore and turned it upside down, so we wouldn't (or couldn't) put it back in easily. After Pauls Dad left one of us got onto the top of the boat, it was very slippery and hard to stay on but after a while (and a few bruises) we all finally mastered it, except for "ole weird Harold" he just sat on the end of the boat a flapped his arms like some sort of bird. We played all sorts of neat-o peachy-keen games like "King of the boat top" "I can stay up longer than you can" And "Ha Ha You can't knock me off 'cause I' can stay on longer" But all in all it was real B-O-R-I-N-G.

	1	2	0

9 They are having fun jumping on the boat they might be playing boats and got caught in a storm and they found an un explored island and they were far far from any other land and they tried to make a boat to get off the island and the boat fliped over and thats why there are standing on the boat like that tring to get back and one of them said, "lets swim back were are not very far so they swam back to the island and tried to make a fire out of twigs so they could dry out and that was a real problem but they had more problems than that there were indians on the island and were ready to attack and if the people

were attacked that would be the biggest problem to the people that just came back and they were real tired and couldn't move very fast and thats why they are jumping up and down.

13   There was some kids jumping on a overturned boat. Boy how I wish I was playing with them they were having fun if I was there I would of had lots of fun. I hope none of them gets hurt. I like to see kids have fun. It's better than getting in trouble. What If the owner of the boat comes and see them playing. I hope the boat dosen't go into the water and then tips over. I hope that girl on the end dosen't fall into the water.

   Good-by kids see you tomorrow

                           1   2   1
9   they are paying on the boat I wish I could play but I had my good clothes on my mom said don't go out and get dirty she said watch them play on the boat they are haveing lots lots of fun we are going out to eat one boy is jumping onther is seating on the boat
   the End

13   You should get off that boat because one of you might get hurt. or the boat may fall in the water and you all might be KILLED or something so lets not play here and lets go some where more safe for no one can get hurt becaust that happened to me and it isn't no laughing matter I could have been killed so thats why I don't want none of you to share my experence so lets leave before it Does Happen because I don't want such young kids to die so early in Life

17   See that little girl standing on the end of the boat? Thats my little sister, Beth. She looks like shes having a fun time with her friends. They all live around here and are all very mischievious. They are always geting in trouble for the things they do. Theyre not being mean or ugly or anything, its just that little kids, being little kids sometimes get into things they should'nt.

   Actually, they should'nt be playing on top of the boat because theres mud all around the boat and any minute one of them is going to fall off the boat & into the mud, but they have to fall off the dock before they get to the mud, but it won't be long. . . .

   I knew it! There they go, right off the dock and into the the mud. (chuckle, Chuckle)

   Beth! You'd better stay out of the mud! Mom'll get mad!

   One thing about kids though they can never stay clean for long and never mad at each other long. Why, just yesterday Beth and Bobo got into a fight as to who should be the princess in the game they were playing. Beth and Bobo finally compromised and said the could be twin sisters and they were happy then.

   Are kids great?

   Tommy is a happy kid. He always is happy and is always busy doing something. Tommy, Beth, Tim and Bobo always through the football around or play tag together. Usally its just the four of them but a new boy just moved in the block so he's started hanging around with them now. They all have a good time and usally amuse themselves by doing the simplest things.

	1	2	3

17 I would of said get off that boat if he wouldn't of got off I would go over there and get him off I hate to see anyone get hurt. But I wouldn't let any of my friends get hurt.

	2	1	0

9 We are have fun on the boat. What if I mother catch us playing on the boat. But we might fall in the lake and my mother will kill her self. I am going before I fall in the lake. You chicken and the kept on meling. So one boy fell in the lake and got dranded. All the others kid ran home crying and they mothers ask them whats wrong my friend fell in the lake. you all did't have any buines down I am going to whoup you when your daddy gets here. I am going to tell hill and for him to whoup you again. Mother please dont let daddy whoup me. I want do it any more Then I will ponish you. All the other kid did't get no whoupen. They got to go back and play.

	2	1	1

17 Whee, isn't this fun. Lets imaging we're outcast pirates. Jump for that sail, tie the brigging. This is our faithful ship, sailing over the tropical seas. Feel the strong, salty wind whisking over your face! I can almost feel the waves moving under our feet. Now all jump up! There we just missed getting dunked by that big breaker. How's the weather up their at the top of the crows mast, Jack. Just fine? Good. Now lets be off on our way on another adventure. Lets go to the arctic this time. Bu, its geting mighty cold now. Look! Theres a giant whale! Lets spear him and take it back to our homeland. I can even hear its heaving lungs. Closer, closer, now. Good, we got her. Pull her in. What, she's pulling us. Hold on! Pull harder! Wow, we're gaining speed. Wheres she going to take us? Whats going to become of these poor lost souls in this perilous situation. Well stay tuned to this program, next week for further adventures. Same time, same channel! See you now; this is the hearty Kaptin Kidd signing off now. And remember, if you bad breath and rotten teeth use goopy. Coopy brand tooth paste is the most fantastic product now on the market. If your eyes look kind of soupy, use goopy.

Now that was fun, what shall we do now. Sail for fantistic Australia well its off now!

	2	1	2

9 I am going to tell about if I was on the top of th boat. playing. one day me and my friends went playing there were six of us and we wanted to go down to the lake and so we did we went Down to the lake and we saw a boat and it was tiped over and they wanted to go play on it and so they did But I told them not to But they didn't Listen so I Just went on walking But then Sandy Shelly Sherri Kim and Renee called out to me and said hey Lori come on so I went over there and said ok But just for a Little while and so I Just played for a little While and then I said I am going to go home now and I said to my friends hey you guys are you comeing

and they said ok and so we went home and we were heard something and the boat fell in and they ran to see what happend and I said to them see If you didn't come you would of been in the water come on I said lets go home and so we went home and they never went down by the lake by there selves and neather did I

The end

                    2   2   1
9   These kids are jumping on a boat. I said be careful." You might get hurt.
Don't push! Everybody could have a chance. Take it easy. Why don't you
want him to play too. He could play. If you could play he could play! Why
don't you ask him. If you won't ask him I will. Do you want to play. I ca'nt my
mother do'nt want to play with people I do'nt know. Where is you mother.
She is over there. I'll ask her could your son play. Would you take care of him.
Sure I will take car of him. Ok! He could play! Thank You! Do you want to
play jumping! Ok! Kids you got a new freind! We do! His name is John!

                    2   2   2
17   Sunday afternoon I was taking a walk along the lake and I came across five
kids playing on an overturned boat. I stopped to watch them, and they were
having so much fun I wished I was one of them. It really took me back to
when I was little, those days were so carefree. At first they were playing a
modified version of King-on-the-mountain, modified to fit the boat. One boy
was a little bigger than the rest and usually was king, except when he lost his
blaance, or footing. As young children usually do they soon lost interest in this
game and began skipping rocks across the lake to see which one could get it
to go the farthest. After the "victor" was established they went on to a game I
never seen anyone play before. They turned the boat upright and did a sort of
dance inside it. I have no Idea why they were doing it but it was fun to watch
all the same. Finally they tired of playing with the boat and started playing
"Ring-a-round-the-rosie's". Now this was a game I could understand, and I
longed to be part of. After about 5 minutes went by I finally got up enough
courage to go and ask them if I could join them. *they said sure* so I did. And
you know I don't think I've had so much fun in years!

                    2   2   3
9   I would go over to them and ask them if I can join them and I would ask them
what they are playing   I would play that game with them   we
would have fun playing with each other. I would say be careful you might fall
and hurt yourself They would say we are playing a game and we are having
alot of fun playing the game with each other.

Writing Task: Primary Trait Scoring Guide for "Woman's Place" Essay

Some people believe that a woman's place is in the home. Others do not. Take
ONE side of this issue. Write an essay in which you state your position and defend
it.

ENTIRE EXERCISE

    0   No response; fragment

    1   Does not take a clear position, or takes a position but gives no reasons
        Restatement of stem
        Position given then abandoned

Position confused, or not defined at all
Position given, no reasons for it
Note: Taking a "middle of the road" position is acceptable

If a lady wants to work she should be able to "cos of womans lib.

A woman's place is not at home because I know she wouldn like to be at home all the time doing housework everyday, but if she has kids she would have to pay somebody to watch them, that's if she had a job.

I believe that a woman's place is in the home. Women need to stay home and take care of their house. If a woman has children she should be home spending time with the kids. If a woman is home she has more time to clean the house, cook and prepare meals. I think the man of the house should be able to support his wife. She should not hurt his pride by working.

I think that a woman who have kids should be at home. The woman sould take carry of the home and the kids and her men. If the woman do not have any kids I think the woman can go out and get a job if she wants to.

Women should stay home and clean their house. What I mean there better off at home washing dishes washing clothes and etc. Some of the Women know a days just want to get out of the house and want to know what's happening lately around their neighborhood. for that they should'nt have gotten married!

In the money situation it doesn't really bother me if my husband gets more than me. It all goes to the same thing. If I weren't married and I were doing the same as a man. I think we should be paid the same. If we could do the same equal things.

I believe that a womens place is where ever she wishes it to be just so she is happy with what she does and is good at it.

I believe that a woman's place does not necessarily have to be in the home. Women who would rather pursue a career in a variety of different fields should be granted the opportunity to do so. They should not have to feel obligated toward becoming a good housewife if they have other interests. Women who have the intelligence, drive, and courage should use these qualities to become involved in any area of work they desire. Men must give them this right.

I think that a woman's place is in the home. I don't think that women should have to work. Its OK I wouldn't mind it. If a women wants to work which some do. Thats fine. But if you have children I think you should stay at home with them. If its necessary to work then I guess that you have to work.

2 Takes a position and gives one unelaborated reason

I do not believe that a woman's place is in the home. Women shouldn't have to stay home all day cooking and cleaning, just because they're women. All human beings should be treated equal and this includes a well-educated woman being able to work at a job, instead of doing menial housework tasks all day.

"A woman's place is in the home", also sounds to me me like to be a woman you have to be married. If women weren't educated and couldn't get a job then single woman would have to marry to survive?

I velieve that the woman's place is in the home only when the man of the house is capable in providing a comfortable size income. I believe then if the man can't provide, the woman should go out and help this man. Also a woman's place is in the home when there is little children, like from ages newborn until let say 2 to 3 yrs. of age, when they most need the comfort and the love of the mother.

I think that a woman should do what she wants if she wants to say home she can do the housework. If a woman have children and he husband is dead there is not another person in the house that can do any work so she has to go out get a job and do the best that she can to do to support her family.

I think a woman should work in a home becuase she knows want to do.

I think that a women place is at home. I don't think a women should have to work in a factory unless people don't have enough money to live on. A women should be at home with her kids. A women at work don't have enough time to spend with her kids, or her family and clean house like it should be. A women at work don't have much time to do what she wants.

3   Takes a position and gives one elaborated reason, one elaborated plus one unelaborated reason, or two or three unelaborated reasons

A womans place is not at home she has the same right to have a job and work. No woman should be at home all the time. Most women can do the same work as men. Some women are as strong as men.

I say that this really depends upon the individual but I don't agree with this statement. I feel that if a woman can work and wants to work that she should. This way she can also help her husband out with some of the bills or what ever. Also the women won't always have to depend on her husband for money to spend on herself or him like for a gift.

I believe that a womans place is not in the home. I feel that if a woman wants to work that this is her right as long as she can take care of the children in the family. As long as a lady can perform her job adequelly let her work. Woman can be just as reliable as men, but they can't do the physical jobs that men can do. That is why I feel women can work and that their place is not in the home. If they can find a job let them work.

I beilive that a woman's place is at home because it would be easier on her to stay home and clean house, cook the meals and take care of the children if any. A working woman is usely easiler to be tired or ran down and taking care of the home too. She might not even have time for husband or children maybe even her home by trying to hold down a job. She wouldn't have time to take care of herself as she normally would or to have kids.

One should not generalize about "a woman's place" *because* like men, a woman should have the choice of her profession. Being a housewife is like any other full time job which should be chosen by the individual. Keeping women in one profession is like telling all men to do the same job. In this way, our society would not be well rounded or prosper because of the imbalance. Women are human beings like men and should be given the full right of choice.

I believe that a women should go to work. The money she'd make at a full time job would compensate for day care of her children plus leaving her money to help with the weekly needs, banking account, or some other emergency fund.

I agree with the statement that a woman's place is in the home. For many years this has been a major social issue. Yes, the issue of women's rights and equality in a man's world has plagued us since Atom and Eve. I say that if we are to survive in the future the woman should stay in their own domain where the belong, in the home. If a hard working man gets home and has no nutrition waiting for him, then how is he to live. If he cannot live and function, then how will his job get done. And if his job is not done, then what about other men and their jobs. If this should come about then how is our strong nation, dependent on our men, going to survive in the future.

4   Takes a position and gives two or more elaborated reasons, one elaborated plus two or more unelaborated reasons, or four or more unelaborated reasons

Women do belong in the house for many reasons. If women aren't in the house who would do the cleaning? If the woman went to a job everyday she would just have to give up her paycheck to restaurants for food, the cleaning lady, and to a laundry for her dirty clothes. If the lady of the house stayed home she'd probably do a better job cleaning her house because it is her own. Anything that's your own, you take better care of it. When the woman of a house goes to work it often puts great pressure on her to do all the chores of the house plus her job. This could cause many family arguments and splitting of families.

If she didn't work, she could take care of the children, house, etc., but think of the additional income that she is missing. I'm sure that if she had a job, it could very well cover the expense of a cleaning women, maid or some sort of house keeper as well as child care-taker. As long as the woman is working, it relieves much tension and harder work from the other part (husband). As a result he might even be able to work as many hours as the woman or the woman work as much as the man. In either case, there would be a positive outcome at the end.

A woman's place is not in the home. Woman are human beings, it is their God given right to pursue what ever career they desire. Life, liberty and the pursuit of happiness have been mentioned in the Declaration of Independence yet women have been denied their rights in this sexist society. Not everyone wants to do the same job or pursue the same goals, must women be limited to a narrowly defined sphere of activity? No, a resounding no! We are people, human beings with as complex mental, emotional, physical needs as men, a fact ignored. We are regarded as the second sex, the incomplete sex, satisfied and made whole only by a family. And it is this false assumption shared by many men and women too, fostered by the society we live in that has destroyed many lives because people were not allowed to express the full range of their God given gifts and creativity. This attitude has been, is reinforced at every turn and what seem to be the most trivial points are often the most telling because they "go without saying". A fine example would be that in filling out the front cover, we are identified as female by number 2. These slights are equivalent to the demigration of Blacks in Westerns where the villains always wear black hats.

7   Illegible, illiterate

8   Misunderstands the question

9   I don't know; I don't want to do it; any reason given for refusing to write a response

Note: Score points 5 and 6 were not used for scoring this exercise.

APPEALS

CONVENTIONAL WISDOM

1   Contains this type of appeal

We are regarded as the second sex, the incomplete sex, satisfied and made whole only by a family

People label her

Even in the Bible the scriptures show that the woman is in the home

Stereotyped as "the weaker sex", women have endured prejudice endlessly

I think this is just because the husband has always been known as the bread winner

2   Does not contain this type of appeal

PERSONAL EXPERIENCE

1   Contains this type of appeal

I'm not used to having my mom at home all the time

A woman was promoted to seargent in the police. she was in the patrol car the a police man. A bunch of ruff bys were loittering a patrolman got out and the guys startting beating him up the lady sergent sat in the car and just screamed

I saw a woman driving trucks, buses even trying to clean off the streets and sidewalk

2   Does not contain this type of appeal

But I know that if I had no kids I would take a job to have a little of my own money

AUTHORITY

1   Contains this type of appeal

If God would of wanted us to be the same he would of given us the strength he gave men to do

Many famous American authors have said woman can take life better than men

Also, in recent scientific discoveries, the woman's new position

2   Does not contain this type of appeal

ANALOGY OR FIGURATIVE LANGUAGE

1   Contains this type of appeal

Such duties should never be left for one person alone because that would be like a skunk in a daisy field—breaking up the beauty of marriage

Russia is a good example of equality for women, more women are Doctors and women work in steel factories and do manual labor. Women are Road Repair workers. Russia sent the first Women in to space

2   Does not contain this type of appeal

HISTORY

1   Contains this type of appeal

Also, look at the contributions Martha Mitchell has made. If she had lost her courage and remained a happy homemaker we would still believe everything Pres. Nixon would be saying and Watergate would still be a hotel, not an incident

Taking the dilema in Israel, if the former premeir, Golda Mier had not come out of her shell, where would this country be

Suppose great women like Mary McLead Bethune had stayed in the home

Women such as Marie Curie, a scientist, have helped a great deal in treatments and research in many fields of science

History has shown that when a women strays from home she gets herself or someone else in trouble. Look at Helen of Troy. She didn't stay at home and she starts a war

Mrs. Nighengale, she a famous women in her days. Mrs. D an England school teacher taught at the first public college

If Woodrow Wilson's wife has stayed at home who would have taken his place in office, and Franklin D. Roosevelt must have thought his wife's place was by his side because he asked for Advice instead of using the presidential cabinet for advice

Women have been fighting for equality for a long time and I feel just as sure about the subject as Lucretia Mott, Lucy Stone, or Elizabeth Cady Stanton

2   Does not contain this type of appeal

LEGAL RIGHTS

1   Contains this type of appeal

   Either way which ever women prefer, to do she has the right to do so

   They have a right just as men to go out and work

   Each human being has the right to do what he or she wants to do

2   Does not contain this type of appeal

   But if they should get equal rights, that means that the ones that do not support it will have to suffer to

   I feel that if a woman wants to work that is her right, as long as she can take care of the children in the family

   Every woman should have just as much right to work as a man

PURPOSE OF APPEALS

1   Appeals advanced in own cause

2   Appeals to refute opposing position

3   Appeals both advancing and refuting

4   No appeals given

Bibliography

Britton, James. *Language and Learning*. Coral Gables, Fla.: University of Miami Press, 1970.

Diederich, Paul B. *Measuring Growth in English*. Urbana, Ill.: National Council of Teachers of English, 1974.

Kinneavy, James. *A Theory of Discourse*. Englewood Cliffs, N.J.: Prentice-Hall, 1971.

Mellon, John C. *National Assessment and the Teaching of English*. Urbana, Ill.: National Council of Teachers of English, 1975.

National Assessment of Educational Progress. Writing Reports no. 3 (1970), no. 5 (1971), no. 8 (1972), no. 10 (1972), no. 11 (1973), 05-W-01 (1975), and 05-W-02 (1976).

Looking at a piece of student writing, we can make judgments about both the appropriateness and the maturity of word choice or diction. Appropriateness is a matter of the particular relationship among writer, audience, subject, and the purpose the writer is trying to achieve. Our judgment about the appropriateness of a writer's diction depends almost entirely upon our sense of this relationship. Judgments about maturity of diction are another matter. We are no longer primarily concerned with the relationship among speaker, audience, subject, and purpose. We are interested, rather, in the probability of a given word's appearing in the discourse of writers of different ages. In the following chapter, Patrick Finn shows how the computer can give us very precise characterizations of the maturity of word choices in a piece of writing by comparing the writer's choices to standard word frequency indexes. Finn conjectures about how students, teachers, and researchers might be able to use this kind of information about writing.

COMPUTER-AIDED DESCRIPTION OF MATURE WORD CHOICES IN WRITING

Patrick J. Finn

The Computer and Evaluation of Writing

Two convictions frequently held by teachers of writing regarding the use of the computer in evaluating writing have a devastating effect on communication. One conviction is that the computer can, and someday will, replace human evaluators and do a better job of evaluating writing. People holding this belief begin to read a discussion like the one presented below with high hopes that the day has arrived. When they see at some point that what is being suggested will not replace human raters (thereby relieving them of an onerous task), they stop reading and are disappointed. Such readers should be forewarned that this paper contains no proposal that will replace human evaluators of student writing.

The second conviction is that writing is a product of intelligence and creativity and that a computer cannot evaluate this product. A corollary to this conviction is that suggestions to evaluate writing by computer are symbolic of a basic struggle between engineers and humanists. Readers holding this conviction may be assured that this chapter does not propose that a computer evaluate themes. A computer cannot evaluate themes; it cannot even add numbers. Adding is an intelligent process. A person can wire a computer so that holes punched in cards (representing numbers) will close certain electrical circuits and cause a number to be printed which will be the same number a person would write if he or she were adding. But the computer is not adding. Circuits are simply opening and closing within the computer because a person designed the circuits to do so under specified conditions.

In this chapter I will propose some ways of making *judgments* about word choices. These judgments are based on human observations about the nature of language in general and the nature of the writing of individuals; some deductions can be made from these observations. But first, a great deal of counting of word frequencies is necessary. The computer, receiving and transforming electrical impulses, will print the same lists and numbers as a person who is counting words, but the computer can produce the lists and numbers in a minute fraction of the time it would take a human to do so. Therefore, the computer is not making judgments or evaluating anything; it is simply a tool.

When *any* suggestion is made (involving the use of the computer or not) regarding the improvement of teaching writing, responding to writing, evaluating writing, etc., someone is dissatisfied. If one person proposes a way of diagnosing spelling difficulties, another says "Yes, but it doesn't improve paragraph structure." When a speaker proposes a way of enhancing student creativity, there is the inevitable "Yes, but it doesn't improve spelling." This chapter describes and responds to *only one* component of students' writing—word choices.

Earlier Exploration into Using the Computer to Evaluate Writing

In an article entitled, "The Imminence of Grading Essays by Computer," Ellis Page (1966) argued that some features of written language can be measured by computer, and he proposed that it is reasonable to determine grades for students' essays on some of these variables.

Page coined the words *proxes* (for "approximate variables") and *trins* (for "intrinsic variables"). For example, there is an intrinsic feature of writing which we may call "syntax complexity." One may reason that persons who produce more complex syntax are apt to use more prepositions and subordinating conjunctions than persons who produce less complex syntax. A computer can be programmed to produce a list of prepositions and subordinating conjunctions found in writing. Here is a variable which is intrinsic in writing, and a second variable which one can program a computer to tabulate. Page proposes that such tabulations of the prox (the number of prepositions and conjunctions) reflect the true value of the trins (syntax complexity).

Page (1968) demonstrated that grades arrived at by computer tabulation of some 30 proxes (e.g., sentence length, number of subordinating conjunctions, average word length in letters) correlated as well with the grades assigned by four human judges as the grades of the four human judges correlated with each other. Slotnick (1972) demonstrated that factor analysis of 34 proxes accounts for six factors which he named Quality of Ideas, Spelling, Diction, Sentence Structure, Punctuation, and Paragraphing.

Slotnick and Knapp (1971) concede that grading by counting proxes does have limitations, but they point out possible applications of computer tabulation which may be more important than assigning grades. For example, the correlation between tabulations of proxes and grades given by human raters may give us valuable insight into the bases of judgment of experienced essay graders. One rater is cited who, upon discovering that his grades correlated more highly with proxes associated with vocabulary than those proxes associated with syntax, claimed to have been surprised by this finding and said he gained a heightened awareness of his own processes in evaluating themes as a result. Secondly, computer tabulation might be regarded as a source of data analogous to having a second reader. Finally, computer tabulation might be put into a format which would suggest possible problems in an essay directly to the student writer. These suggestions might be used as a basis for rewriting *before* the theme is handed to the instructor for evaluation.

These three suggestions—(1) heightening awareness of intrinsic variables to which human evaluators may respond, (2) using the computer tabulations to check on evaluation as one would use a second reader, and (3) presenting tabulations *to the student* as suggestions for possible rewriting—are more relevant to this chapter than the notion of actually assigning grades based on computer tabulation.

The following demonstration of how these suggestions may be implemented is based on a set of student themes which were written on a single assigned topic. This demonstration is not meant to be definitive but illustrative. What appears to be useful here might not be entirely appropriate with themes on a different topic. However, it will be argued that the techniques employed are valid and generally applicable, even if the details might need adjusting as the topic of the written sample changes.

The Sample

A set of 101 essays written by students in the Rochester, New York area forms the basis for this discussion. The themes were collected as part of a project directed by Thomas R. Knapp and reported by him at the annual meeting of the American Educational Research Association in 1972. The stimulus for the themes was as follows:

> Imagine that a large company near you has been found to be seriously polluting a local river. Some people have been talking about closing the company down until something can be done about the pollution. If the company is closed down, many people will be out of work. Write your feelings about whether to shut down the company. Be sure to indicate *why* you feel the way you do.

The themes were written by boys and girls in grades 4, 8, and 11. Some statistics describing the sample follow. Note the distinction between the word *tokens*, the total number of words, and the word *types*, the number of *different* words.

	Grade 4	Grade 8	Grade 11	All Themes
Number of Themes	36	34	31	101
Number of Tokens	2,818	5,852	6,134	14,794
Number of Types	592	912	1,145	1,817

Knapp (1972) warns that this is a "grab sample," meaning that the sample was not scientifically chosen to represent fourth, eighth, and eleventh graders. For his purposes a representative sample was not necessary. He also states that there was attrition in the original sample particularly because of the inability of some students to write on the assigned topic. Therefore, this sample probably represents the better fourth-grade students and the more cooperative eighth- and eleventh-grade students.

These themes are satisfactory for the present discussion because this is not a report of an experiment; it is a discussion of some principles of word frequency with suggestions for how these principles might be employed in the *analysis* of students' word choices. A representative sample of themes would probably reveal more striking differences between grades and better demonstrate the feasibility of using these principles for *evaluation*. However, establishing norms for word choices is only suggested here and is not represented as an accomplished fact.

Two themes from this sample, each followed by an alphabetical list of word types appearing in the theme, follow. In several respects Theme B is superior to Theme A, but for the purposes of this chapter, only the word choices will be considered. Theme B yields what appears to be a more mature list of word types than Theme A. But this is a subjective judgment. The task set forth in this project is to devise a way of making more precise and objective statements about comparative maturity of word choices as exemplified in Themes A and B.

Theme A: Grade 4

Types: 72   Tokens: 141

I think they shouldn't because the people need jobs to support there family. That is why we have poor people is either because of there color or they didn't go to school. More and more people are moving they need jobs badly. Look at the people in Rochester that just hang around because they have no money because there Black. All of the white people blame them for stealing the money that they need for there family or some of them steal it for dope or drinking money. The people are polluting in the river and killing fish. Why can't they put it in something so that it didn't pollute the water. Now we can't get clean fish and eat the fish because they have grease or something else. We see fish floating on the lake because they pollute in the water.

all	eat	it	or	steal
and	either	jobs	people	stealing
are	else	just	pollute	support
around	family	killing	polluting	that
at	fish	lake	poor	the
badly	floating	look	put	them
because	for	money	river	there
Black	get	more	Rochester	they
blame	go	moving	see	think
can't	grease	need	school	to
clean	hang	no	shouldn't	water
color	have	now	so	we
didn't	I	of	some	white
dope	in	on	something	why
drinking	is			

Theme B: Grade 11

Types: 72   Tokens: 101

People have been protesting against the evils of industry since the 18 hundreds. I think that it is very unnatural, unsafe, and also unhuman to pollute any river with illsmelling dye or any other form of industrial waste. So feeling this strongly against pollution I would form a group, an antipollution group and get the support of some local critics and put into action some means of closing down the company. If this does not work then I think I would call for the government to help to correct the abuse. And would advocate a new system of purifying the water.

a	critics	if	people	the
abuse	does	illsmelling	pollute	then
action	down	industrial	pollution	think
advocate	dye	industry	protesting	this
against	evils	into	purifying	to
also	feeling	is	put	unhuman
an	for	it	river	unnatural
and	form	local	since	unsafe
antipollution	get	means	so	very
any	government	new	some	waste
been	group	not	strongly	water
call	have	of	support	with
closing	help	or	system	work
company	hundreds	other	that	would
correct	I			

Mature Word Choices and Word Frequency

If one panel of judges was asked to choose the words from Theme B that indicated maturity on the part of the writer, and the second panel was asked to choose the words from Theme B which were comparatively uncommon words in English, they would probably compose the same list. It would include the words *abuse, advocate, antipollution, critics, evils, illsmelling, pollute, pollution, purifying, support,* and *unnatural.*

Again, if one panel of judges was asked to choose Theme A or B as the theme reflecting more maturity of word choice and a second panel was asked to choose Theme A or B as the theme having more uncommon words, both panels would probably choose Theme B.

Word frequency has been used as a measure of word "quality" for many years; it has been used to estimate the amount of "work" accomplished by a word (Zipf 1965), the amount of "information" delivered by a word (Cherry 1957), and the degree of "importance" of a word in a text (Luhn 1959). Lorge (1944) reports that Talmudists used word frequency in text analysis over a thousand years ago. The analysis suggested in this paper is based on word frequency as well.

Three large-scale word counts have been done in America by Thorndike and Lorge (1944), Kucera and Francis (1967), and Carroll, Davies, and Richman (1971). The 1971 word frequency list is used in the study reported here. Carroll, Davies, and Richman tabulated word frequencies in a corpus of over five and a half million words drawn from over a thousand textbooks used in American schools in 1969. The study reports not only the actual number of times each word appeared, but also the distribution of the word by grade and school subject. Since the sample was drawn by a sophisticated statistical technique, the authors were able to estimate the probability of each word's occurrence in a theoretical sample of *all* textbooks. This estimate is reported as a Standard Frequency Index (SFI). If a word has an SFI of 90, one would expect to find it once in every ten words. (The word *the* has an SFI of 88.6.) If a word has an SFI of 80, one would expect to find it once in every 100 words. (The word *is* has a standard frequency of 80.7.) The SFI in increments of ten, the probability of appearance in an indefinitely large sample, and an example word appear in Table 1.

Words having low SFI's are not bizarre words. Using frequencies to identify mature word choices is not equivalent to looking for freakish vocabulary or words whose meanings are known to a highly select group. When I refer to words as uncommon, the qualification *relatively* uncommon is always intended.

If the relationship between mature word choices and word frequency were uncomplicated, a person would merely have to find the word frequency for each word in a theme, average this frequency (the sort of judgment-free tasks for which computers are useful), and compare themes for average word frequency. This would constitute an objective measure reflecting relative maturity of word choice. Unfortunately, this relationship *is* complicated. Other factors affect word frequency besides "difficulty" and other factors affect word choices besides "maturity."

When these other factors are recognized and accounted for, however, the knowledge of frequencies becomes very useful in identifying maturity in word choices.

The first source of complication is that students write rare words for reasons other than maturity. One reason is that most topics *dictate* the choice of certain words. If the assignment calls for a discussion of the relationship between pollution and employment, which is what our sample calls for, it would not be surprising to find words like *company, factory, jobs, pollution,* and *waste* on the papers of the most immature students. It is difficult to imagine a paper being written on this topic without some of these words, but these are not highly frequent words. Their SFI's are as follows: company, 58.0; factory, 56.0; jobs, 56.1; pollution, 43.6; and waste, 54.9.

The question then becomes, how does one identify words that are demanded by the topic of the paper and therefore do not indicate maturity of word choice regardless of their SFI. Information scientists (Luhn 1959; Carroll and Roeloffs 1969) are asking essentially the same question when they ask how word frequency information might be used to find a list of words in a text that ought to be included in an index. Luhn was the first to suggest a very simple solution. If a word is very rare in the language and it appears repeatedly in a book, it is probably essential to the book's topic and should appear on the index. For example, the word *diesel* (SFI=42.4) is expected to appear about once in 900,000 words. If *diesel* appears ten times in a ten thousand word chapter, it is probably a very important word in the chapter and should appear on the book's index. Of course, tabulating a word's appearances in a chapter and finding its SFI on the list can be done in seconds with the aid of a computer. Luhn called words identified in this manner "Key Words."

Exactly the same reasoning can be applied to students' themes. If a word is quite infrequent in the language and appears repeatedly in a set of themes, the word is probably intimately related to the topic. For example, one would expect the word *environment* (SFI=55.4) to appear once in about 50,000 words and *pollution* (SFI=43.6) to appear once in about 700,000 words. In the 14,794 word tokens in the sample, *environment* appears 14 times and *pollution* appears 148 times. Obviously, the use of the word *pollution* is dictated by the topic and the use of the word *environment* is strongly suggested by the topic. Rather than use the term "Key Word," which has been used to name several concepts over the years, the term "Topic Imposed Words" will be used to name the class of words discovered in students' themes using the concept explained in this paragraph.

Table 1

Interpretation of the Standard Frequency Index

SFI	Probability of the Word's Occurrence in a Theoretical Indefinitely Large Sample	Example of a Word with Designated SFI
90	1 in every 10 words	the (88.7)*
80	1 in every 100 words	is (80.7)
70	1 in every 1,000 words	go
60	1 in every 10,000 words	cattle
50	1 in every 100,000 words	quit
40	1 in every 1,000,000 words	fixes
30	1 in every 10,000,000 words	adheres
20	1 in every 100,000,000 words	cleats
10	1 in every 1,000,000,000 words	votive (12.7)

*Where no word has the designated SFI, the SFI of the closest word appears in parentheses.

Table 2

Topic Imposed Words

Word Type	SFI	Frequency in Sample
company	58.0	191
pollution	43.6	148
factory	56.0	98
polluting	33.7	61
jobs	56.1	51
shut	56.7	50
companies	54.5	29
clean	59.7	28
closing	52.5	26
polluted	44.2	23
rivers	58.7	17
pollute	37.1	16
unemployment	43.0	16
factories	56.5	14
seriously	52.0	14
waste	54.9	14
workers	58.6	14
cause	59.4	12
sewage	45.9	12
killing	51.5	10
lose	56.8	10

The Relationship between the Assigned Topic and Mature Word Choice

How rarely must a word appear (how low an SFI must it have) before it is "very rare"? How often must it appear in a book before it is thought to appear repeatedly? In indexing, as in identifying Topic Imposed Words, the answer may vary. One advantage of using a computer is that one can try out combinations of values until the list of words appears to fit the concept of Topic Imposed Words. The list of Topic Imposed Words in Table 2 was derived by finding words which have an SFI of less than 60 and which appear at least ten times in the entire set of themes.

The list appears to have face validity. All the words seem to be suggested by the topic and those having higher frequencies in the sample appear to be demanded by the topic. It would be possible to refine the analysis of Topic Imposed Words if it served one's purpose. For example, the words *waste* and *sewage* appear in eighth- and eleventh-graders' themes, but not at all in fourth-graders' themes. It might be useful for some purposes to identify words which the topic suggests to older students but not to younger ones. However, to keep the present discussion manageable, the Topic Imposed Words in Table 2 will not be further analyzed.

The basic premise of this discussion is that word frequency can be used to identify mature word choices. This simple relationship is not demonstrated by simply averaging word frequencies of mature and immature writers; there are complicating factors. One is that some rare words may be chosen by immature writers because the topic demands using these words. When such words are identified and sorted out, the relationship between word frequency and maturity of choice becomes clearer.

Low Frequency Words that Do Not Indicate Maturity

Classes of words that are rare in print, but do not reflect maturity or sophistication, are a second complicating factor in the relationship between word frequency and maturity of choice. These classes of words become apparent when rare words (SFI less than 50) are identified in the themes of fourth graders. Only fifty such words appear on fourth-grade themes. Eight of these words (16%) are proper nouns. It is probably the highly specific referent, a unique property of proper nouns, which makes these words rare. Slang words, such as *dope, fake, junk, messy, skinny*, and *stinks*, make up a second class of rare words used by fourth graders. These words are so highly informal that they are not apt to appear in print—particularly not in textbooks. Contractions, such as *isn't, can't*, and *wouldn't,* make up a third class of words having low SFI's but not reflecting maturity. The informality of contractions causes these to be rare in print but fairly frequent in students' writing.

If we eliminate "Mature Word Choices" from Tables 3 and 4, that is, words with an SFI of less than 50 but which are not Topic Imposed Words, proper nouns, contractions, or slang, we would discover that eleventh graders produced 241 Mature Word Choices and the fourth graders only 34. The words themselves, plus the fact that seven times as many such words are produced by eleventh graders as fourth graders, are offered as evidence that this category of words is aptly named.

Table 3

Words on Fourth Grade Themes
Having SFI's of Less than 50

bake	donation	junk	Ontario	smartly
bud	dope	kills	payed	someplace
Burman	dump	Leo	pills	stealing
cleaner	empties	lima	reverse	stinks
clubhouse	expense	Lisa	Rochester	sues
complain	fake	manages	ruining	tractor
complains	Freddy	messy	seaweed	transfer
complaining	Freddy's	mit	sediment	volunteer
crabs	grease	mow	self	wells
destroying	Janie	nay	skinny	worrying

Identifying Words that Do Not Discriminate between Grade Levels

The words in Table 5 were identified by searching for word types that appear on themes from each of the grades in the sample, 4, 8, and 11. Many of these words are function words. Those that are not function words are so common that their use in a theme does not suggest maturity on the part of the writer. In earlier drafts of this chapter, these words were called Non-discriminators, indicating that their use did not discriminate between mature and immature writers. However, it is probably true that the proportion of words in a theme that appear on this list will discriminate. Themes with larger proportions of these words will be written by less mature writers. Therefore, this class of words is called "Undistinguished Word Choices." The list in Table 5 is offered as the best evidence that words appearing at all grade levels constitute a cohesive set and that this set is properly named.

Table 4

Words on Eleventh Grade Themes
Having SFI's of Less than 50

abuse	controversial	gals	minute	Sandy's
accepting	corrected	gee	minutes	Sarah's
adequate	correcting	Genesee	modified	selfish
advances	corrections	genuine	Mom	severely
advise	crisis	gross	multitude	Sherwood
advocate	critics	guilty	naked	shutdown
agencies	damaging	gutters	neglect	shutting
agrees	deadline	halted	nitty-gritty	sights
aiding	dealt	halting	nonchalant	signing
algae	decline	hardship	nowadays	smarter
allotted	deduct	hazards	offending	solving
alright	definitely	heaven	opposing	specialists
alternatives	dependence	hinder	ourself	specifications
ample	deceased	hippy	overall	springing
analyze	designing	holders	ownings	stake
Andrews	disastrous	homeowners	participated	starve
anticipate	discharge	how's	personally	statesmen's
antipollution	disgusted	hurting	petition	suds
arises	disposal	ideological	philosopher	suicide
assignment	disregard	ignored	pollutants	swaying
assure	drain	ignorant	pollutes	talkers
assured	drastic	ill-smelling	possibilities	technicians
availability	dye	illustrates	potential	temporarily
awhile	earning	imposed	preservation	temporary
backing	Eastman	improvement	preserve	terribly
Ballentine	ecology	incoming	pressurized	thereby
basically	egotist	incomplete	presumably	there's
beaches	eighty	inconvenient	priority	Thompson
bug	eliminating	inflation	profit	throws
builds	employ	inform	proposals	trash
burden	employees	innocent	prospects	ultimatum
butts	employers	inquire	prosper	undersigned
cares	employing	instrumental	protesting	unemployed
Catherine	endangered	insurance	punishing	unfortunate
cheaper	enforcing	investigating	purifying	unhuman
chicken out	entails	irritated	Rd.	uninhabitable
Cindy	environmental	irritating	reactions	unnatural
citywide	estimation	jeopardize	relevant	unorganized
closes	eventual	jobless	realist	unsafe
coatless	everything's	justify	recycled	unusable
commit	evils	K.	refuse	versus
compensating	facilities	Kay	refuses	voters
complain	fade	Kodak	regulations	wastes
complaining	fails	layed-off	replacing	waterway
compliances	failures	litter	representative	well-planned
conceivably	financial	logical	reputations	wildlife
concerns	filter	long-range	researchers	worsen
confessed	filters	Marlene	resolves	wrecks
consequences	finance	menace	ripples	wrongs
consideration	fined	merit	ruins	Xerox
contribute	forbid	mess	rusty	You've
controlling	funds	minded	salvage	

Table 5

Undistinguished Word Choices

a	doesn't	house	no	take
able	doing	how	not	talking
about	done	I	now	that
again	don't	if	of	that's
air	down	I'm	off	than
all	drink	important	on	the
also	dumping	in	once	their
and	each	into	one hundred	them
animals	earth	is	open	then
another	either	it	or -	there
any	else	its	other	they
anything	enough	job	our	thing
are	even	just	out	things
around	every	keep	over	think
as	everyone	kill	own	this
ask	everything	know	part	time
asked	fair	lake	pay	to
at	family	lakes	people	too
away	feel	let	person	try
bad	few	like	place	until
be	filter	little	plants	up
because	find	live	problem	us
been	first	living	put	use
before	fish	long	rather	very
being	fishing	look	reason	want
better	food	lot	right	was
big	for	make	river	water
build	form	making	run	way
business	from	man	running	we
but	get	many	said	well
buy	getting	may	same	what
by	give	maybe	save	when
call	go	me	say	where
called	going	mean	see	who
came	good	men	should	why
can	got	might	since	will
children	had	money	so	with
cleaning	happen	months	some	without
clear	happy	more	someone	won't
close	hard	most	something	work
closed	have	much	soon	worked
come	having	must	source	working
could	he	my	start	world
couldn't	health	near	stay	would
day	help	need	still	years
did	him	never	stop	you
didn't	his	new	support	your
do	home	next	swim	

Describing and Responding to Individual Themes

The task proposed at the beginning of this chapter was to describe an objective system that would enable one to compare the word choices used in Themes A and B. In the preceding section several classes of words were identified among all the word choices made by all the 101 students in the sample. All of these classes were identified empirically, except the classes Slang, Contractions, and Proper Nouns. I feel that these classes would be reliably identified by judges; if this system were to be applied, a panel of judges might be used to check the judgments of the experimenter, particularly for the class Slang. Once these classes have been identified and lists created, one can classify words on individual themes in seconds with the aid of a computer. The words in Themes A and B have been so classified. The analysis appears in Tables 6 and 7. Although A is longer, both themes used 72 different words. (Theme A repeated words more often, creating a longer theme. The relationship between the number of word types and the number of word tokens has been explored elsewhere as a method of recognizing maturity in writing. See Fox 1972.) Student A uses more Undistinguished Word Choices, more Contractions, Proper Nouns, and Slang, and fewer Mature Word Choices. The two students use the same numbers of Topic Imposed Words and Unclassified Word Choices.

Perhaps with a set of a thousand themes instead of one hundred, norms could be established for the proportion of Undistinguished Word Choices, Mature Word Choices, Topic Imposed Word Choices, etc. Possibly the norms could take into account grade level and length of theme. One might do the same sort of thing with ten different topics so that a student being evaluated could choose a topic and so that the same student could write on different topics on different days to get a more reliable measure of word choices.

Furthermore, the rank ordering of papers and comparing of papers to norms on the dimension of word choices are useful for purposes other than simply assigning grades. A theme may have so many usage problems, for example, that the evaluator is blinded to other components of the writing. The proposed analysis permits the evaluator to look at word choice in isolation and may permit him or her to discover a strength in the theme or perhaps to consider strategies for improving word choices as a response to the writer.

For example, the analysis of Theme A suggests that some specific attention might be given to the maturity of word choices. Is the student aware that in expressing opinions in writing, a slightly less informal tone would be more convincing to most readers? Writing out *cannot, did not,* and *should not* would add to the formality of the paper. One might ask, "What word would a writer in *The Weekly Reader* have used instead of *dope?*"

Table 6

Word Types Sorted by Objectively Defined Categories

Theme A: Grade 4	Theme B: Grade 11
Types: 72 Tokens: 141	Types: 72 Tokens: 101

Undistinguished Word Choices

all	is	see	a	if	some
and	it	so	also	into	support
are	just	some	an	is	that
around	lake	something	and	it	the
at	look	support	any	new	then
because	money	that	been	not	think
either	more	the	call	of	this
else	need	them	does	or	to
family	no	there	down	other	very
fish	now	they	for	people	water
for	of	think	get	put	with
get	on	to	have	river	work
go	or	water	help	since	would
have	people	we	I	so	
I	put	why			
in	river				

Contractions, Proper Nouns, Slang

can't	(none)
didn't	
dope	
Rochester	
shouldn't	

Topic Imposed Words

clean	closing
jobs	company
killing	pollute
pollute	pollution
polluting	waste

Mature Word Choices

grease	abuse	ill-smelling
stealing	advocate	protesting
	antipollution	purifying
	correct	unhuman
	critics	unnatural
	dye	unsafe
	evils	

Table 6—*Continued*

Theme A: Grade 4		Theme B: Grade 11	
Unclassified Words			
badly	hang	action	industrial
block	moving	against	industry
blame	poor	feeling	local
color	school	form	means
drinking	steal	government	strongly
eat	white	group	system
floating		hundreds	

Table 7

Comparison of Word Categories
Represented on Themes A and B

Category	Theme A		Theme B	
	Number of Types	Percentage of Types	Number of Types	Percentage of Types
Undistinguished Word Choices	47	65	41	57
Contractions, Proper Nouns, Slang	5	7	0	0
Topic Imposed Words	5	7	5	7
Mature Word Choices	2	3	13	18
Unclassified Words Choices	13	18	13	18
Total Words	72	100	72	100

A very common failing in student writing is a lack of relatedness or consecutiveness of ideas—the quality of writing that rhetoric manuals refer to as "coherence." Lack of coherence springs from the writer's failure to see that the reader has a different mind from the writer's and, therefore, the connections between the writer's ideas must be made explicit. It is very difficult to get a writer who suffers from this difficulty to understand what the trouble is.

A teacher might discuss this very difficult concept of coherence with a student by testing his Unclassified Words against the question, "How is this word, as used in the theme, relevant to the stated purpose of the theme (in the case under discussion, the assigned topic of the theme)?" The student who wrote Theme A might be asked how the words *color, black, white, drinking, moving, school,* and *steal* are relevant to the topic. He might be made to see that the connections among race, schooling, employment, and factory closing are not made explicit in this paper. The student might either be able to develop the logic of his argument, or he may see that he has responded to a question about economics with a stereotyped generalization and has failed to analyze the real question.

This writer could be helped to build on a very weak paper. By eliminating contractions and slang and by making explicit the socio-economic relationships he only hints at in the paper, he could develop a superior paper.

Theme B, on the other hand, is a coherent theme. One is struck by the appropriateness of this writer's Mature Word Choices and Unclassified Words. However, a person experienced with the technique and with the topic might notice something missing from these word categories. *Earning, employ, employees, financial, funds, hardships, income, inflation, jobless, layed-off, starving,* and *unemployed* are examples of Mature Word Choices used by other writers on this topic. The presence of these words indicates that some writers have considered the plight of those who will lose their jobs if the factory closes. The absence of these words from Theme B calls attention to a fact that might have otherwise gone unnoticed: This writer has not considered the problem of the unemployed and has, therefore, ignored half of the assignment.

Another fact revealed by considering word choices in isolation is that Theme A uses words referring to people 17 times (*family,* twice; *people,* six times; *them,* twice; and *they,* seven times). Theme B uses the word *people* once, which, along with the other references to people (*group, critics,* and *government*), is an impersonal, abstract reference. It is beside the point whether Theme A or Theme B is superior because of the kinds of words used to refer to people. The point is that the analysis proposed here makes such observations more probable and gives the evaluator avenues of response to students' writing that are not otherwise apparent.

Creating a Topic Specific Data Base

I have shown that words relating to unemployment and words relating to people can be identified on an *ad hoc* basis by using the objective word analysis to respond to themes of individuals. It is possible to make such observations a standard part of the word choice analysis once we have observed that the presence or absence of certain categories of words might direct the attention of the writer or the teacher in useful ways.

The analysis of the themes might be done as follows: 1) The themes are typed onto IBM cards. 2) A computer is programmed to process all the themes and print an alphabetical list of all the types used, followed by the Standard Frequency Index (taken from the *American Heritage Word Frequency Book* list on computer magnetic tape), the frequency of the word type on all themes, and the frequency of the word type in grades 4, 8, and 11. (See Table 8.) By simple arithmetic, lists can be compiled of Topic Imposed Words, Mature Word Choices, and Undistinguished Word Choices; by a quick scanning of the list, a judge can identify contractions, proper nouns, and slang terms.

But scanning the alphabetical list of types, particularly after the Topic Imposed Words and Undistinguished Word Choices are eliminated, one is struck by the fact that there are other classifications of words which seem to reflect maturity, but which require intelligent and subjective judgment. For example, in the present sample, the following categories of words appear to reflect maturity of word choice on the part of the writer: Abstract nouns (e.g., *alternatives, efforts, evils, menace, reasons, suicide*); verbs that indicate cognitive activity rather than physical activity (e.g., *abuse, blame, complain, investigating, manage, support*); adjectives which reveal a judgment on the part of the writer regarding an abstract state (e.g., *adequate, controversial, drastic, genuine, potential, unnatural*).

If judges were to scan the alphabetical list of types produced in a hundred themes and identify Abstract Nouns, Verbs Denoting Cognitive Activity and Adjectives Judging an Abstract State, the words that were reliably classified could make up semi-objective lists which would define useful categories for describing word choices. A data base could then be created to identify each of the approximately 1800 words produced in these 100 themes as in Table 8.

A data base of this sort could be used to describe word choices of students who are not included in the sample but who are asked to write a theme on the same topic. If Theme B had been written after the data base had been compiled, the analysis would have revealed that this theme has five abstract nouns (*action, government, means, support, system*) and four verbs denoting cognitive activity (*correct, form, help, think*). However, the words *evils, abuse, advocate, feeling, unhuman, unnatural,* and *unsafe* would not be in the data base since they do not appear in the sample outside of Theme B. The computer could be programmed to find the SFI for these "Unique Words" and print them out with a few words of context from the theme so that they could be classified by the analyst. These new classifications could be added to the analysis in Table 6.

Sets of themes on specified topics might be sent by a teacher to the data processing office of the school district. The themes would be typed onto cards and submitted to the computer which would be programmed to count words in a theme, match words to appropriate lists in the data base, find the SFI of the words it does not find in the data base and print the word types in each theme in appropriate lists, and finally print a list of words that are in the theme but not in the data base, with the SFI and the context in which the word occurs in the theme. An analyst would then classify the new words, type them into a terminal, and obtain a new analysis.

Table 8

Data Base for First Twenty-Five Word Types in Sample

Word Type	SFI	Frequency				Objective Categories	Semi-Objective Categories
		All	Gr4	Gr8	Gr11		
a	83.9	308	40	135	133	Undist.	
able	63.7	21	4	8	9	Undist.	Abstract Adj.
about	73.8	62	8	33	21	Undist.	
absolutely	50.7	1	0	0	1		
abuse	40.0	1	0	0	1	Mature	Cognitive Verb
accept	54.5	1	0	0	1		Cognitive Verb
accepting	45.4	1	0	0	1	Mature	Cognitive Verb
achieved	51.4	3	0	0	3		Cognitive Verb
act	59.2	1	0	0	1		
action	59.4	6	0	3	3		Abstract Noun
actions	53.1	2	0	0	2		Abstract Noun
actually	59.3	2	0	0	2		
addition	60.2	1	0	0	1		Abstract Noun
adequate	46.6	2	0	0	2	Mature	Abstract Adj.
advances	48.9	1	0	0	1	Mature	
advise	46.7	2	0	1	1	Mature	Cognitive Verb
advocate	40.6	1	0	0	1	Mature	Cognitive Verb
affected	52.4	2	0	0	2		
affecting	44.6	1	0	1	0	Mature	
afford	51.9	3	2	0	1		Cognitive Verb
after	70.6	13	0	7	6		
afternoon	59.6	2	0	1	1		Abstract Noun
again	68.5	10	1	7	2	Undist.	
against	65.1	4	0	1	3		
age	60.7	2	0	2	0		Abstract Noun

In high schools and colleges students might have access to computer terminals or keypunch machines and type their own themes into computer readable form on a fairly regular basis, assuming there was a data base for a variety of writing assignments. The computer could be programmed to write out messages showing discrepancies between the student's theme and norms developed for that grade level. The student might use the suggestions for revisions.

For example, the computer might be programmed to receive themes and to print out questions like the following under specified conditions:

—Have you considered the problem of unemployment in writing your theme?

—Would your argument be more convincing if you used *cannot* instead of *can't?*

—Is the word *pollote* spelled correctly?

—You use the word *workers* seven times. Could you combine some of the ideas about workers into the same sentences?

—You have used the word *they* eleven times. Is the reference always clear?

For themes written to fulfill different assignments, the computer might be programmed to write the following questions under specified conditions:

—Have you told what the boy in the picture is thinking?

—Have you described the setting for this story?

—Can you make the relationship between your ideas clearer by using such words as *although, however, but,* or *therefore?*

If the analysis is to be used by the teacher rather than given directly to the student, the message might reflect the basis of observation as well as the suspected problem. For example:

—An extraordinarily high proportion of Mature Word Choices. Check for slang and/or a tendency to overwork vocabulary at the expense of clarity or simplicity.

—Very few Topic Imposed Words. Has the student written on the assigned topic?

—Extraordinarily high proportion of pronouns. Is reference always clear? Might sentence combining be in order?

—Few Cognitive Verbs. Many action verbs. Has the student discussed the motivation of the characters?

The kind of data base suggested for the topic discussed in this chapter could be developed for any number of topics. Word categories used in the data base would vary from theme to theme. One can imagine a theme topic where adjectives denoting duration (e.g., *constant, extended, frequent, lingering, prolonged, repeated, sustained*) or mental states (*cheerful, furious, gloomy, happy, sober, weary*) would constitute a class of words identifying mature themes. With some topics the categories based on word frequencies might be highly discriminating between mature and immature writers, while with other topics these categories may not be very discriminating. With some topics the semi-objective categories verified by a panel of judges may be easily identified and highly useful in suggesting ways to improve themes; with other topics such categories might not be obvious or highly useful.

The techniques outlined here should be tried with many, many topics, and those topics which lend themselves best to these techniques should be used to generate data banks (using 1000 themes rather than 100, perhaps). This may help a classroom teacher, a language arts diagnostician, a researcher in language development, or a school evaluating institution like the National Assessment to isolate, analyze, and organize one component of writing, *word choices*, in order to respond to that component more consciously, more intelligently, and with heightened sensitivity.

Bibliography

Carroll, John B.; Davies, Peter; and Richman, Barry. *Word Frequency Book.* Boston: Houghton Mifflin, 1971.

Carroll, John M., and Roeloffs, Robert. "Computer Selection of Keywords Using Word-Frequency Analysis." *American Society for Information Science Journal* (1969):227-33.

Cherry, Colin. *On Human Communication: A Review, a Survey, and a Criticism.* Cambridge, Mass.: MIT Press, 1957.

Fox, Sharon E. "Syntactic Maturity and Vocabulary Diversity in the Oral Language of Kindergarten and Primary School Children." *Elementary English* 49 (1972):489-96.

Knapp, Thomas R. "Essay Topics and Modes, and Their Effects on Student Prose." Unpublished paper. Rochester, N. Y.: University of Rochester, 1972.

Kucera, Henry, and Francis, W. Nelson. *Computational Analysis of Present-Day English.* Providence, R. I.: Brown University Press, 1967.

Lorge, Irving. "Word Lists as Background for Communication." *Teachers College Record* 45 (1944):543-52.

Luhn, H. P. "The Automatic Derivation of Information Retrieval Encodements from Machine Readable Texts." *Documentation and Library Science* 3 (1959):1021-28.

Page, Ellis B. "The Imminence of Grading Essays by Computer." *Phi Delta Kappan* 47 (1966):238-43.

_____. "The Use of the Computer in Analyzing Student Essays." *International Review of Education* 14 (1968):210-25.

Slotnick, Henry B. "Toward a Theory of Computer Essay Grading." *Journal of Educational Measurement* 9 (1972):253-63.

Slotnick, Henry B., and Knapp, John V. "Essay Grading by Computer: A Laboratory Phenomenon?" *English Journal* 60 (1971): 75-87.

Thorndike, Edward L., and Lorge, Irving. *The Teacher's Word Book of 30,000 Words.* New York: Bureau of Publications, Teachers College, Columbia University, 1944.
Zipf, George K. *Human Behavior and the Principle of Least Effort: An Introduction to Human Ecology.* New York: Hafner Publishing Co., 1965.

Recent research in syntax has given us a precise, comprehensive description of the development of syntactic ability through the school years and of the possibilities of syntactic fluency in the writing of publishing professionals. The two names most often associated with this research are Francis Christensen and Kellogg Hunt. Within the classroom, teachers are learning to use this research, along with other insights from transformational-generative grammar, for formative evaluation, demonstrating to student writers the possibilities in their writing for various embeddings, conjoinings, substitutings, and loose, additive modifications. Teachers are also beginning to use special materials which provide intensive sentence-combining practice for students, practice which produces marked increases in their syntactic fluency.

In this chapter Kellogg Hunt reports recent research which confirms findings from his initial research of the 1960s. His new findings will reassure teachers and researchers of the usefulness of key syntactic structures for describing writing performance and measuring growth in writing.

EARLY BLOOMING
AND LATE BLOOMING
SYNTACTIC STRUCTURES

Kellogg W. Hunt

For a dozen years now I have been interested in describing the syntactic structure of the sentences produced by schoolchildren as they pass from the early grades to maturity. The children and their sentences obviously do mature, and the more we know about the process, the more we can hope to help them in their writing, and perhaps also in their speaking and reading and thinking. If the description of such a process is comprehensive enough, that description becomes a scientific theory, a model. It can then be tested in unanticipated ways, and thus be either confirmed or disconfirmed by the data obtained with the new procedure. In this chapter I will present certain new data that bear upon an earlier theory, confirming it at certain points and refining it at still other points.

My first studies (Hunt 1964, 1965, 1967), like other studies of the sixties and before, worked on a large body of writing, one thousand words from each student. For a fourth grader to write a thousand words sometimes took a whole school year. This writing was on whatever topic the children happened to be concerned with in the normal course of their schoolwork. The writing was free of any control from me, the investigator, including subject matter and style. I will refer to such writing hereafter as *free writing*.

Since completing those two studies in the 1960s, I have conducted two other studies (Hunt 1970, and 1974 unpublished) using a carefully controlled method for eliciting writing from students of different ages. I call this kind of writing *rewriting*, in contrast to *free writing*. Obviously it is a special kind of what we ordinarily think of as rewriting. A student is given a passage written in extremely short sentences and is asked to rewrite it in a better way. Once this is accomplished, the researcher can study what changes are made by students at different grade levels.

There are several advantages to this procedure. For one thing, since all students rewrite the same passage, all students end up saying the same thing—or almost the same thing. What differs is how they say it. Their outputs are strictly comparable. The differences are unmistakable, so a smaller corpus of writings can be used. A second advantage of the re-writing technique is that students can be confronted with specific syntactic problems which the investigator wants them to handle. To discover their method of handling an unusual problem in their free writing, the investigator might have to wade tediously through a vast corpus. A third advantage is that a student's syntactic maturity can be tested with a re-writing instrument in less than a class period, but to get a representative sample of a fourth grader's free writing would take many hours.

There is, of course, a danger in generalizing from a single rewriting instrument. The results obtained will depend to some extent on the prob-lems set. Insofar as the investigator sets an abnormal task he or she will get an abnormal result. These results need to be checked against free writing. For instance, in one of the rewriting studies, not one of the 250 students participating, some of them twelfth graders of superior IQ, produced a single noun clause. But in another rewriting study, covering comparable age groups, noun clauses were produced with an average frequency of about one per student. There is nothing mysterious here. The difference in the outputs was determined by the difference in inputs. One instrument provided abundant opportunity for the production of noun clauses; the other provided none. We predicted that difference when we designed the two instruments.

In order to review two of the claims I made in the sixties about syntac-tic maturation, I must first introduce the term "T-unit." The easiest way to explain what I mean by this term is to use examples. My favorite example is the following passage written by a fourth grader. As you will see, this fourth grader wrote intelligibly enough—even forcefully—but he didn't punctuate at all. He wrote all this as a single sentence.

> I like the movie we saw about Moby Dick the white whale the captain said if you can kill the white whale Moby Dick I will give this gold to the one that can do it and it is worth sixteen dollars they tried and tried but while they were trying they killed a whale and used the oil for the lamps they almost caught the white whale.

Now let me cut this passage into its T-units. I will define a T-unit as a single main clause[1] (or independent clause, if you prefer) plus whatever

---

[1] A clause is defined here as a subject (or coordinated subjects) with a finite verb (or coordinated finite verbs).

other subordinate clauses or nonclauses are attached to, or embedded within, that one main clause. Put more briefly, a T-unit is a single main clause plus whatever else goes with it. Here is the passage reprinted, with each T-unit numbered and beginning a new line.

1 I like the movie we saw about Moby Dick the white whale
2 the captain said if you can kill the white whale Moby Dick I will give this gold to the one that can do it
3 and it is worth sixteen dollars
4 they tried and tried
5 but while they were trying they killed a whale and used the oil for the lamps
6 they almost caught the white whale.

As you read those T-units, you may have noticed that each one is a grammatically complete sentence, regardless of the fact that one begins with *and* and another with *but*. (Of course they are grammatically complete; each contains a main clause.) You may also have noticed that they are the shortest stretches of wordage that the passage can be cut into without creating some fragment. (Of course they cannot be reduced further; each contains only one main clause.) For example, if we cut the first of these into two pieces, one of the pieces would be a fragment.

I like the movie (grammatically a sentence)
we saw about Moby Dick, the white whale (grammatically a fragment)

Perhaps it would be safe for us to think of T-units as the shortest grammatically complete sentences that a passage can be cut into without creating fragments—but it is safe to do so only so long as we remember that two main clauses must be counted as two T-units. The T in T-unit stands for "terminable." Grammatically, a T-unit can be terminated with a period or other terminal mark.

The reason for defining a T-unit, as distinguished from a sentence, is simply that the T-unit turns out, empirically, to be a useful concept in describing some of the changes that occur in the syntax of the sentences produced by schoolchildren as they grow older. When we know what a T-unit is, we can understand certain measures of maturity that we could not understand without it.

On the basis of my studies of free writing in the sixties, I made two broad claims. One was that as schoolchildren get older, the T-units they write tend to get longer, measuring length as the mean number of words per T-unit. This claim might be called the T-unit length hypothesis. To get the mean T unit length of the passage already analyzed, one simply counts the total number of words (in this case 68) and divides it by the number of T-units (in this case 6, giving a score of 11.3). The score for any other passage would be arrived at in the same way.

The T-unit length hypothesis is easy enough to prove true or false. All one has to do is get a representative sample from a school population of one age and another from a comparable population of another age and compute the scores for the two samples. If the score for the older group is larger, then that evidence tends to confirm the claim; if not, then that evidence tends to disconfirm the claim. So many researchers have found that their evidence tended to confirm the claim, that I suppose it is now accepted by all persons who know about such matters.[2]

A second broad claim which came from my study of free writing in the sixties is that as schoolchildren get older they tend to consolidate into their T-units a larger and larger number of what transformational grammarians call S-constituents. An S-constituent is something abstract, not something concretely and tangibly observable like a word. Roughly speaking, an S-constituent is the abstract structure that underlies the simplest of sentences—what used to be called kernel sentences. Several S-constituents may underlie a single sentence of ordinary complexity. For instance, in *Aspects of the Theory of Syntax* (1965), Chomsky indicated that three S-constituents underlie the sentence "The man who persuaded John to be examined by a specialist was fired." One S-constituent would be the abstract structure underlying "Someone fired the man." A second would underlie "The man persuaded John." A third would underlie "A specialist examined John." My claim was that as schoolchildren grow older, they consolidate a larger and larger number of such S-constituents into their actual T-units. We might call this the "number of consolidations" hypothesis.

Since S-constituents are abstract and theoretical, it is not possible to prove or disprove this hypothesis easily and directly like the other one. Nonetheless, it is an interesting experiment to study how schoolchildren consolidate, not abstract S-constituents which underlie extremely simple sentences, but extremely simple sentences themselves.

That is what a rewriting instrument can show. And now we will look, in some detail, at the changes made by schoolchildren on the first six sentences of the "Aluminum" passage. Here are those six.[3]

1   Aluminum is a metal.
2   It is abundant.
3   It has many uses.

---

[2]Various extensions and refinements to the claim have been made. One of the first (Hunt 1967) was that T-unit length tends to vary with mental age, not just chronological age. Another (O'Donnell, Griffin, and Norris 1967) was that T-unit length in speech as well as writing tends to increase with age. Another (Pope 1974) is that T-unit length for fourth graders varies somewhat with the mode of discourse.

[3]The "Aluminum" passage can be found in its entirety at the end of this chapter.

4　It comes from bauxite.
5　Bauxite is an ore.
6　Bauxite looks like clay.

How would students of different grade levels rewrite this passage?

A typical output of a fourth grader is printed in the right-hand column below. The input is reprinted in the left-hand column.

1　Aluminum is a metal.	Aluminum is a metal and
2　It is abundant.	it is abundant. It has
3　It has many uses.	many uses and it comes
4　It comes from bauxite.	from bauxite. Bauxite is
5　Bauxite is an ore.	an ore and looks like clay.
6　Bauxite looks like clay.	

What syntactic changes has the fourth grader made? In the last T-unit he has deleted the subject, coordinating the two predicates. In addition he has put *and*'s between two pairs of T-units. In summary, then, he has coordinated two pairs of T-units and one pair of predicates. That is all.

How would a typical student rewrite these same six input sentences four years later, that is, as a typical eighth grader? His output is printed in the right-hand column below.

1　Aluminum is a metal.	Aluminum is an abundant
2　It is abundant.	metal, has many uses, and
3　It has many uses.	comes from bauxite.
4　It comes from bauxite.	Bauxite is an ore that
5　Bauxite is an ore.	looks like clay.
6　Bauxite looks like clay.	

The eighth grader takes the predicate adjective of the second input and makes it a prenominal adjective, *abundant metal*. He coordinates three predicates, inputs 1, 3, and 4. He transforms input 6 into a relative or adjective clause. He does not coordinate any full T-units.

To avoid tedium, I will not show how a typical tenth grader or even twelfth grader would rewrite this. Instead, see how a typical skilled adult, someone whose articles appeared in *Harpers* and *Atlantic*, would rewrite it.

1　Aluminum is a metal.	Aluminum, an abundant
2　It is abundant.	metal with many uses
3　It has many uses.	comes from bauxite, a
4　It comes from bauxite.	clay-like ore.
5　Bauxite is an ore.	
6　Bauxite looks like clay.	

This typical skilled adult transforms the predicate adjective of input 2 into a prenominal adjective, *abundant metal*, as did the eighth grader. He reduces input 1 to an appositive, *Aluminum, an abundant metal*. He changes the verb *has* from input 3 to the preposition *with*. He changes the predicate *looks like clay* into the modifier *clay-like*. He transforms input 5 into a second appositive, *bauxite, a clay-like ore*.

Looking back at these three sample rewritings, let us see whether they tend to confirm or disconfirm the two claims made earlier. You will recall that one of the claims made on the basis of free writing was that the number of words per T-unit increased with the age of the writer, at least through twelfth grade, and the number was still greater for skilled adults. Even in our tiny sample of three rewritings we can see this tendency manifest. Our fourth grader produced twenty-five words in his five T-units, for an average of five words per T-unit. The eighth grader produced twenty words in two T-units, for an average of ten words per T-unit. The skilled adult produced thirteen words in one T-unit. So our increase has been from five to ten to thirteen.

This increase is not far off the means in the full experiment, where fifty students out of several hundred from each grade were chosen so that their scores on standardized tests would represent a normal distribution of scores from high to low. The grades chosen were 4, 6, 8, 10, 12, a total of 250 schoolchildren. In addition, out of a number of authors who recently had published articles in *Harpers* or *Atlantic*, twenty-five rewrote the passage. They are here called skilled adults. Furthermore, twenty-five of Tallahassee's firemen who had graduated from high school but had not attended college rewrote the passage too. They will be called average adults.

For this larger population of 300 writers in the "Aluminum" study, the words per T-unit increased at every two-year interval, the difference being significant at the .01 level. Here are the figures for G4, G6, G8, G10, G12, average adults, and skilled adults: 5.4, 6.8, 9.8, 10.4, 11.3, 11.9, 14.8. Notice that average adults are only a little above twelfth graders, but skilled adults are far above both groups.

So there is no doubt that the rewriting study tends to confirm the claim about T-unit length. How about the other claim—the one about the number of S-constituents or simple input sentences? Our fourth grader consolidated the six input sentences into five main clauses, five T-units. Put the other way around, we could say that his five T-units are derived from six input sentences, six S-constituents. The average for his five T-units, then, is six divided by five, or one and one-fifth (1.2) input sentences per output T-unit. The eighth grader consolidated the same six input sentences into a mere two T-units, so we could say that the average for him is six divided by two, or three input sentences per output T-unit. Where the fourth grade score is about one, the eighth grade score is about three. The skilled adult consolidated all six inputs into one output T-unit. So we would score him six input sentences per output T-unit.

To review, then, the fourth grader's score is about one; the eighth grader's score is three; the skilled adult's score is six. These scores increase with age, so the samples, which are fairly typical of the rewritings from a large number of carefully selected subjects in the full experiment, provide data that tend to confirm one claim of the theory.

For these 300 writers, a tabulation of their 10,000 input-output structures indicated that the number of input sentences per output increases at every age level, just as the theory would predict. Here are the scores for G4, G6, G8, G10, G12, and skilled adults: 1.1, 1.6, 2.4, 2.8, 3.2, 5.1. Notice that skilled adults are almost as far above twelfth graders as twelfth graders are above fourth graders.

When studying free writing, a researcher sees only the output. The input lies hidden in the writer's head. Its presence is conjectural and can only be inferred. But in rewriting, one sees both input and output equally well. Neither is conjectural. So the results of the rewriting instrument are critical to the theory, and, as we see, they support both of the claims.

So far in this chapter I have supported the claim that successively older students can consolidate a successively larger number of simple sentences into a single T-unit. Usually when writers consolidate, they employ some sentence-combining transformation. They reduce one of the sentences to something less than a sentence, perhaps to a phrase or a single word. Now we will look at certain of these syntactic changes to see which ones are used commonly even by the youngest writers, which are used commonly only by middle grade writers, and which are used commonly only by the oldest writers. Thus we can separate the early blooming syntactic structures from the later blooming and even the latest blooming structures.

At the outset we noticed that our fourth grader joined two pairs of his T-units with *and*'s. He did so with grammatical correctness. He put his *and*'s in the right place, at the boundaries between the T-units. He knows where those boundaries come. But hereafter he will learn to do this less often. Young children do it correctly but profusely. Older writers do it correctly but parsimoniously. In the "Aluminum" passage a typical fourth grader coordinates 20 pairs of T-units; a typical sixth grader about half as many, 9; a typical eighth grader, 6; a tenth grader about 3; a twelfth grader maybe 2; and a skilled adult 1 or 2 for an average of 1.6. So we see that T-unit coordination blooms early, immediately starts to die, but lingers on for years, being gradually smothered by its relatives.

Coordination between predicates blooms early too, but it fades very little thereafter. Our fourth grader coordinated two of them, our sixth grader coordinated three, but our skilled adult knew too many better things to do. Typically, the number of coordinated predicates increases a little from G4 to G6 and then drops off slightly. For the large sample the actual frequency is 1.9, 2.2, 2.2, 2.0, 2.0; for average adults 1.9; for skilled adults 1.6. The number of opportunities to coordinate predicates is 26, but no one took more than about a tenth of these opportunities.

Can we say anything more about growth in coordination with *and*? Perhaps a little. Consider what we might expect to be a slightly more difficult problem. Here are two adjoining input sentences:

23 It contains aluminum.
24 It contains oxygen.

Here both subjects are the same, so we might delete one of them and get a coordinated predicate:

It contains aluminum and contains oxygen.

But both verbs are the same too, so we might delete both a subject and verb and get coordinated objects:

It contains aluminum and oxygen.

This is the more mature construction.

Almost all of the writers in grade six and older used this more mature construction, deleting both the subject and verb. But among the youngest group, the fourth graders, almost half deleted nothing at all, and of the remaining half more chose the less mature construction. So even within coordination using *and*, there are grades of maturity: least mature is to delete nothing; more mature is to delete the subject; most mature is to delete both subject and verb.

Another fairly early bloomer grows out of inputs like one and four:

1 Aluminum is a metal.
4 It comes from bauxite.

Our skilled adult consolidated these two by deleting *is* from the first sentence and making it an appositive:

Aluminum, a metal, comes from bauxite.

He also made an appositive out of another pair.

4 It comes from bauxite.
5 Bauxite is an ore.

This became

. . . comes from bauxite, an ore.

The "Aluminum" passage provided two more pairs of sentences that invited appositives to be formed. Ability to write appositives was in full bloom by grade eight, but not by six or four. Here is the number of appositives produced by successively older grades: 1, 8, 36, 30, 34.

But not all transformations are in full bloom as early as coordination and the appositive. For instance, look at these two inputs:

    1 Aluminum is a metal.
    2 It is abundant.

Our eighth grader moved the adjective *abundant* out of its predicate position in the second sentence and put it in front of the noun *metal* in the first sentence.

    Aluminum is an abundant metal.

Thus two T-units become one larger T-unit.

The "Aluminum" passage provided six pairs of sentences like this, inviting a predicate adjective to become a prenominal adjective in some adjoining input sentence. The fourth graders performed this transformation 13 times, sixth graders 66 times, eighth graders 140 times, tenth graders 212 times, and twelfth graders 223 times. Here we have the strongest kind of evidence of a steady increase in transformational facility. This transformation blooms more and more profusely with age.

Our skilled adult did something else that the younger writers did not do. Consider the second of these two sentences.

    5 Bauxite is an ore.
    6 Bauxite looks like clay.

Half the skilled adults changed the predicate *looks like clay* into an adjective, *claylike ore*. The younger students did not do so nearly as frequently. In fact, the number of occurrences from youngest grade to oldest was: 1, 2, 3, 10, 14. This change begins to bloom only as late as the tenth grade, where the frequency suddenly triples. But even as late as the tenth grade only a fifth of the writers make the change, whereas among skilled adults half do. So this is a late blooming accomplishment. (It probably is not actually a transformation.) What in effect has happened in this change is that the skilled adult has shifted the grammatical category from verb phrase to adjective.

Older students make other syntactic category shifts more readily. For instance, our skilled adult changed the predicate or verb phrase *has many uses* into a prepositional phrase, *with many uses*. Still other older writers changed that verb phrase to an adjective, *useful*. Three-fourths of the skilled adults did one or the other. But only *half* the twelfth graders did; a *fourth* of the tenth graders; a *fifth* of the eighth graders; and only a *twelfth* of the sixth graders. No fourth grader did. So here again we have a highly discriminating measure of maturity, and a relatively late bloomer.

Francis Christensen, in his study of rhetoric, has singled out certain constructions as being particularly indicative of adulthood. One of those appears three times in this sentence which he cites from E. B. White. I have italicized the key words.

> We caught two bass, *hauling* them in briskly as though they were
> mackerel, *pulling* them over the side of the boat in a businesslike
> manner without any landing net, and *stunning* them with a blow on
> the back of the head.

Here we have four verbs with the same subject, all describing the same
event. The input sentences, reduced to their skeletons would be these:

> We caught two bass.
> We hauled them in briskly.
> We pulled them over the side.
> We stunned them.

These four sentences can be reduced to a single T-unit if we get rid of the
repetition of subjects and add *-ing* to the verbs:

> We caught two bass, hauling them in briskly, pulling them over the
> side, and stunning them.

Of the 300 persons who rewrote "Aluminum," not one of them produced
this construction. Out of 10 fourth graders who rewrote "The Chicken,"[4]
not even one produced it. By 10 eighth graders who rewrote it, it was
produced once:

> She slept all the time, laying no eggs.

By 10 twelfth graders this construction was produced twice. Here are
both examples.

> The chicken cackled, waking the man.
> Blaming the chicken, he killed her and ate her
>   for breakfast.

But the university students produced 14 examples. In fact, 9 out of 10
university students studied produced at least one example, whereas only 1
out of 10 twelfth graders had done so. In the little time between high
school and the university, this construction suddenly burst into bloom.
Here are some examples from those 14 occurrences.

> He caught the chicken, *planning* to eat it the next morning, and
> placed it in a pen located below his window.

> The old man caught the chicken and put her in a pen under his
> window *planning* to eat the chicken for breakfast the next morn-
> ing. Early the next morning a sound woke the man, and *looking* out
> the window, he saw the chicken and an egg.

> *Living* alone in his farmhouse, and without any neighbors, there
> was no one for him to talk to, so he passed his days working in his
> garden, growing vegetables and grain. . . . *Thinking* what a deli-
> cious breakfast the chicken would make, he caught her and put her
> in a pen outside his window.

---

[4]Mean T-unit length for "The Chicken" is G4, 6.7; G6, 8.3; G8, 10.2; G10, 10.9; G12, 12.0;
University, 13.0. The passage can be found in its entirety at the end of this chapter.

For our purposes here, this is a long enough list to demonstrate that some syntactic structures bloom early and some late.

It seems likely that this theory of syntactic maturity applies to languages other than English, perhaps even to all human languages. The "Aluminum" study has been replicated in the Netherlands by Reesink et al. (1971). Reporting their findings in *Psychological Abstracts* they conclude, "The similarity between Dutch and American children in syntactic development is outstanding."

Furthermore, an investigation into Pacific Island languages and some Asian languages has begun at the East-West Center in Honolulu (Hunt 1974, unpublished). The rewriting instrument already referred to as "The Chicken," after being found to discriminate significantly between grades 4, 6, 8, 10, and 12 in English, was translated into a number of Pacific Island languages and some Asian languages. Those translated versions were then rewritten by children aged about 9, 13, and 17, who were, for most languages, native speakers of the language tested. So far, papers in Fijian, Indonesian, Korean, Laotian, and Marshallese have been scored for words per T-unit. For each of those languages the scores for the oldest group are distinctly higher than the scores for the youngest. The scores for the middle group lie in between. The papers in Japanese have been scored, not for words per T-unit, but for number of S-constituents per T-unit, and the results for Japanese are almost exactly the same as for English, supporting the theory.

There seems to be no doubt that syntactic maturity, as measured here, can be enhanced by a sentence-combining curriculum. This seems to be definitely established for grade four (Miller and Ney 1968; Hunt and O'Donnell 1970) and for grade seven (Mellon 1969; O'Hare 1973). For grade four, Hunt's curriculum covered seventeen sentence-combining transformations and included many multi-sentence embeddings. Students responded both orally and in writing. They not only combined sentences, as is done, at least hypothetically, in writing and speaking, but they also broke them back down, as is done, again at least hypothetically, in reading and listening. At the end of the year, 335 students in the experimental and control sections were tested in several ways. On the "Aluminum" passage test, the number of input sentences consolidated per T-unit was, for control students, 2.6; for experimental students, 8.3. Such a difference is unquestionably significant, and would have taken about two years more to accomplish had there not been this instruction.

In their free writing, experimental students wrote significantly longer T-units, indicating greater maturity. They also wrote themes about twenty to twenty-five percent longer than those written by students in the control group. These same students were tested to see whether this curriculum affected their reading comprehension. It might be expected that the decomposing of complicated sentences into their underlying component sentences would make students more conscious of the syntactic problems in reading comprehension. The results of the posttesting were far from conclusive and far from complete, but at least the findings were encouraging rather than discouraging. On what Stedman calls a Reading Structure test, the experimental students scored significantly higher than the control students at the end of the year.

The elementary grades would seem to be an especially appropriate place to use a sentence-combining curriculum; the use of many middle-bloomer transformations increases rapidly at this age. Surely it is possible to test whether a transformation can be taught at a certain age by a certain amount of repetition, or cannot be taught at all until later. Burruel, Gomez, and Mey (1974) have already begun to experiment on how to measure the teachability of a certain structure by a certain method at a certain age. Thus they report, for example, "the *who/which* embedding was performed with a 40% error rate on the first day. By the third day, the students had improved, showing a mere 4% error rate. Some exercises, such as the embedding of conjoined adjectives, proved highly resistant to improvement, manifesting a 50% error rate over four succeeding lessons (p. 219)." The kind of information given previously as to which structures bloom early and which bloom late would be preliminary to actual measures of teachability at a given level.

In the mid-seventies, then, the English teaching profession has a theory of syntactic development that covers a broad range of structures. It also has more than one way of measuring progress toward the goal of skilled adulthood. There is also evidence that curricula already known can enhance syntactic maturity and perhaps assist reading comprehension. One might reasonably hope that a period of rich and varied curricular experimentation would now commence. There are not many areas in the language arts where the goals are as clear and as measurable as in this area, and yet where so little experimentation has occurred.

To the present time, the teaching of language has been guided almost exclusively by the rhetorician's intuition. But the theory of syntactic development reviewed here does not rest upon intuition alone; it rests on a solid body of experimental data. Linguistics will be of vastly greater help to language teaching as it begins to be able to make such statements as: "This structure has this meaning in this environment for this reason." Up until now, only rhetoricians have made such statements, but their intuitive perceptions have often been vague. Linguists now are beginning to devote a great deal of attention to the meaning of surface structure differences, to such matters as presupposition and entailment. As they begin to study the relation between syntax and semantics, they are approaching the rhetoric of the sentence. As they do so, they may be able to say less vaguely some of the things rhetoricians have already said. And if they can say them less vaguely, they can say them more teachably. When that happens, we English teachers can be grateful.

The two passages from which some of the exercises in this chapter were drawn follow.

Aluminum

Directions: Read the passage all the way through. You will notice that the sentences are short and choppy. Study the passage and then rewrite it in a better way. You may combine sentences, change the order of words, and omit words that are repeated too many times. But try not to leave out any of the information.

Aluminum is a metal. It is abundant. It has many uses. It comes from bauxite. Bauxite is an ore. Bauxite looks like clay. Bauxite contains aluminum. It contains several other substances. Workmen extract these other substances from the bauxite. They grind the bauxite. They put it in tanks. Pressure is in the tanks. The other substances form a mass. They remove the mass. They use filters. A liquid remains. They put it through several other processes. It finally yields a chemical. The chemical is powdery. It is white. The chemical is alumina. It is a mixture. It contains aluminum. It contains oxygen. Workmen separate the aluminum from the oxygen. They use electricity. They finally produce a metal. The metal is light. It has a luster. The luster is bright. The luster is silvery. This metal comes in many forms.

The Chicken

Directions: Read the story all the way through. You will see that it is not very well written. Study the story, and then write it over again in a better way. You will want to change many of the sentences, but try not to leave out any important parts of the story.

A man lived in a farmhouse. He was old. He lived alone. The house was small. The house was on a mountain. The mountain was high. The house was on the top. He grew vegetables. He grew grain. He ate the vegetables. He ate the grain. One day he was pulling weeds. He saw something. A chicken was eating his grain. The grain was new. He caught the chicken. He put her in a pen. The pen was under his window. He planned something. He would eat the chicken for breakfast. The next morning came. It was early. A sound woke the man. He looked out the window. He saw the chicken. He saw an egg. The chicken cackled. The man thought something. He would eat the egg for breakfast. He fed the chicken a cup of his grain. The chicken talked to him. He talked to the chicken. Time passed. He thought something. He could feed the chicken more. He could feed her two cups of grain. He could feed her in the morning. He could feed her at night. Maybe she would lay two eggs every morning. He fed the chicken more grain. She got fat. She got lazy. She slept all the time. She laid no eggs. The man got angry. He blamed the chicken. He killed her. He ate her for breakfast. He had no chicken. He had no eggs. He talked to no one. No one talked to him.

Bibliography

Burruel, Jose M.; Gomez, Julie; and Ney, James W. "Transformational Sentence-Combining in a Barrio School." In *On TESOL 74*, edited by Ruth Crymes and William Norris, pp. 219-30. Washington, D.C.: Teachers of English to Speakers of Other Languages, 1974.

Christensen, Francis. *Notes Toward a New Rhetoric*. New York: Harper and Row, 1967.

Hunt, Kellogg W. *Differences in Grammatical Structures Written at Three Grade Levels*. Cooperative Research Project, no. 1998. Washington, D.C.: U.S. Office of Education, 1964.

——. *Grammatical Structures Written at Three Grade Levels*. NCTE Research Report, no. 3. Urbana, Ill.: National Council of Teachers of English, 1965. ERIC Accession no. ED 113 735.

——. *Sentence Structures Used by Superior Students in Grades Four and Twelve and by Superior Adults*. Cooperative Research Project, no. 5-0313. Washington, D.C.: U.S. Office of Education, 1967.

——. "Syntactic Maturity in Schoolchildren and Adults." *Monographs of the Society for Research in Child Development* 35 (February 1970).

Hunt, Kellogg W., and O'Donnell, Roy. *An Elementary School Curriculum to Develop Better Writing Skills*. Tallahassee: Florida State University. U.S. Office of Education Grant no. 4-9-08-903-0042-010, 1970. ERIC Accession no. ED 050 108.

Mellon, John C. *Transformational Sentence-Combining: A Method for Enhancing the Development of Syntactic Fluency in English Composition*. NCTE Research Report, no. 10 Urbana, Ill.: National Council of Teachers of English, 1969.

Miller, Barbara, and Ney, James. "The Effect of Systematic Oral Exercises on the Writing of Fourth-Grade Students." *Research in the Teaching of English* 2 (1968):44-61.

O'Donnell, Roy C.; Griffin, William J.; and Norris, Raymond C. *Syntax of Kindergarten and Elementary School Children: A Transformational Analysis*. NCTE Research Report, no. 8. Urbana, Ill.: National Council of Teachers of English, 1967.

O'Hare, Frank. *Sentence Combining: Improving Student Writing without Formal Grammar Instruction*. NCTE Research Report, no. 15. Urbana, Ill.: National Council of Teachers of English, 1973.

Pope, Mike. "The Syntax of Fourth Graders' Narrative and Explanatory Speech." *Research in the Teaching of English* 8 (1974): 219-27.

Reesink, G. P.; Holleman-van der Sleen, S.B.; Stevens, K.; and Kohnstumm, G. A. "Development of Syntax among School Children and Adults: A Replication-Investigation." *Psychological Abstracts* 47:10536.

The renewal of interest in prewriting or invention among contemporary rhetoricians has led to an important contribution to describing and measuring growth in writing: description of the intellectual strategies (or writing strategies) apparent in the written piece. A description of these strategies tells us, and the writer, what decisions the writer actually made in exploring and presenting a particular subject. These decisions are partly matters of diction and syntax, but they also involve more complex matters of classification and contrast, physical context, sequence, change, and focus and change of focus. Replacing vague comments with specifics can lead writers to make substantial revisions involving reseeing and rethinking. Describing these strategies considerably enriches evaluation at a number of levels: diagnosis, formative evaluation in the classroom, and growth measurement.

MEASURING CHANGES IN INTELLECTUAL PROCESSES AS ONE DIMENSION OF GROWTH IN WRITING

Lee Odell

A number of contemporary rhetoricians argue that if students are to improve their writing, they will need to increase their conscious use of certain cognitive and affective processes during the prewriting stage of composition. It is not adequate, these rhetoricians would contend, to teach students to organize and express existing ideas or even to teach them to recognize faulty syllogisms and distinguish between fact and inference. Composition teachers should show students how to explore, sensitively yet systematically, facts, feelings, values, and ideas in order to determine what it is they wish to say in their writing. This point of view is by no means universally held. More traditional rhetoricians such as Martin Steinmann (1975) assume that rhetorical theory and the teaching of composition are concerned only with effective presentation of ideas, not with their formulation. But in recent years several researchers (Rohman and Wlecke 1964; Young and Koen 1973; Odell 1974) have presented some evidence that:

1 Composition teachers can help students increase their conscious use of certain intellectual (cognitive and affective) processes.
2 Instruction in the use of these processes can result in writing that seems more mature, more carefully thought out, more persuasive.

For teachers, this recent body of theory and research helps solve a recurrent problem; it suggests ways of dealing with student writing that seems superficial, imperceptive, unimaginative. But for those who are concerned with describing and measuring students' growth in writing, this work in rhetoric presents new problems: How do we identify the intellectual processes implicit in students' writing? How do we determine whether students are using these processes as fully and effectively as they might?

As with new questions in any field, these pose so many difficulties that it is tempting to avoid asking them if at all possible. And in some cases, we might reasonably give in to temptation. If we are interested in summative evaluations of students' ability to produce writing that has certain characteristics (e.g., persuasiveness, insightfulness), or if we are interested solely in predicting students' success in college, we might not need to identify the processes by which they formulate the ideas or attitudes expressed in their writing. But if we want to make useful diagnoses or formative evaluations of students' writing—that is, if descriptions of students' present writing are to be used in helping them improve subsequent writing—we must have some insight into their use of these processes. In making this claim, I am assuming that:

1   Although thinking is a complex activity, the number of conscious mental activities involved in thinking may not be infinite; the relatively small number of intellectual processes identified by Kenneth Pike (1964 a and b) lets us describe much of what people do consciously when they examine information, attitudes, or concepts.

2   We can identify linguistic cues—specific features of the surface structure of written or spoken language—that will help us determine what intellectual processes a writer is using.

3   In order to improve students' writing, we will have to determine what intellectual processes we want students to begin using, continue using, or use differently; to make this determination, we must have a good sense of how they are presently functioning.

Intellectual Processes and Linguistic Cues

Although discussions of intellectual processes described by Pike appear in a number of places (Pike 1964, a and b; Young, Becker, and Pike 1970; Odell 1973), I have two reasons for illustrating each of these processes rather fully in this chapter. For one thing, these processes manifest themselves in a variety of ways that are not made explicit in other discussions of Pike's work. Moreover, the linguistic cues described below are useful, but occasionally ambiguous; in order to determine the significance of a given cue, one must have a clear understanding of the intellectual processes it may reflect.

Focus. Pike claims that in order to observe, think about, respond to any phenomenon, we have to segment the continuum of phenomena, we have to focus upon distinct units of experience. "Without segmentation of events into recallable, nameable chunks, without abstraction of things as figure against ground, without reification of concepts manipulatable as discrete elements by our mental equipment, man would be inept" (Pike 1964a). This process of segmenting and focusing occurs all the time in movies and television. The camera zooms in to let us see the details of a character's facial expression, then moves back to tell us more about the character by letting us see his or her posture, gestures, clothes. Moving back still further, the camera shows us the character in his or her physical surroundings. We use this process in our own perception of an object, a person in real life, a character in a literary work; we shift our attention so as to focus on those visible details that seem most significant.

We don't always do this consciously, a fact that becomes clear for many of us when we first see a photograph we've taken ourselves. When we snapped the picture of, say, an infant, we were very aware of the toothless smile, the pudgy, rosy cheeks, the charming (to parents, at least) bit of drool on the baby's chin. But on looking at the developed photograph, we see a large expanse of living room carpet, a chair, a corner of a coffee table, and, way in the background, a swaddled object that might possibly be a baby. We did not do with the camera what we had unwittingly done with our mind's eye. We did not move in so that the camera could select the same visual detail that we had been so acutely aware of when we pushed the shutter.

This process of shifting focus and selecting detail is reflected not only in photography but in the syntax of our written and spoken language. If we examine grammatical focus—that is, the grammatical subject of each clause in a piece of discourse—we can learn a good bit about the way the talker or writer is perceiving and thinking. Consider, for example, this passage from *Life on the Mississippi*, where Mark Twain describes the steamboat as it approaches a small town. (Italics in this and subsequent illustrative passages identify linguistic cues to the intellectual process being discussed.)

> . . . *the furnace doors* are open and the fires glazing bravely; *the upper decks* are black with passengers; *the captain* stands by the big bell, calm, imposing, the envy of all; *great volumes of the blackest smoke* are rolling and tumbling out of the chimneys—a husbanded grandeur created with a bit of pitch-pine just before arriving at a town. . . .

Grammatical subjects of several clauses in this passage suggest a succession of camera shots, a sequence of perceptions: the furnace doors, the upper decks, the captain, the volumes of smoke.

George Orwell's essay, "Shooting an Elephant," shows grammatical focus being used in a slightly different way.

> When *I* pulled the trigger *I* did not hear the bang or feel the kick—*one* never does when a shot goes home—but *I* heard the devilish roar of glee that went up from the crowd. In that instant, in

too short a time, *one* would have thought, even for the bullet to get there, *a mysterious, terrible change* had come over the elephant. *He* neither stirred nor fell, but *every line of his body* had altered. *He* looked suddenly stricken, shrunken, immensely old, as though *the frightful impact of the bullet* had paralyzed him without knocking him down. At last, after what seemed a long time—*it* might have been five seconds, *I* dare say—*he* sagged flabbily to his knees. *His mouth* slobbered. *An enormous senility* seemed to have settled upon him. *One* could have imagined him thousands of years old.

As in the Twain passage, some of the subjects in this passage have a single concrete referent, such as *I, he, his mouth*. But several of the subjects in Orwell's passage—*mysterious, terrible change; frightful impact of the bullet; enormous senility*—do not reflect Orwell's visual perception of single details; instead they suggest Orwell's conclusions about what he saw, or his synthesis of individual details.

In argumentative or expository prose, changes in grammatical focus may reflect shifts in perception. They may also indicate a writer's attention to various facets of a complex topic. Consider, for example, the following excerpt from *The New York Times Sunday Magazine* about the construction of the Alaskan oil pipeline.

For more than six years since the discovery of oil on Alaska's North Slope, *the press* has emphasized and *Washington political leaders* have debated the environmental risks. *Alaskans* have been largely preoccupied with the economic impact. But *sparse attention* has been given to one price of the pipeline which can be labeled only with a phrase verging on the macabre; the human toll, a toll measured both in human despair and in injury and death. *The casualty figures* for pipeline-related workers may well turn out to be higher than for any other major construction project in the nation in modern times.

Initially, the writer focuses on those who have commented on the topic—journalists, politicians, Alaskans. Subsequently, he focuses on a significant failure of these commentators, and then on one main aspect of the controversy (*casualty figures*) they have neglected.

Unquestionably, other parts of a sentence can reflect one's segmenting of the continuum of experience. But by dealing only with the grammatical subject of each clause, we simplify our task in analyzing language and still turn up valuable information about the way a speaker or writer is thinking. Moreover, the grammatical subject seems to have a special significance. Changes in grammatical focus not only imply a shift in thinking or perceiving; they also imply a change in direction or commitment for the rest of the sentence. For instance, in describing the elephant's death, Orwell could have written, "The bullet struck the elephant with a frightful

impact." Instead, he said, "The frightful impact of the bullet had paralyzed him without knocking him down." By focusing on *frightful impact*,
he was obliged to make an additional observation (the impact "paralyzed
him without knocking him down."). Similarly, in talking about the essay,
we might say "Orwell opposed imperialism." But if we were to focus on
Orwell's opposition to imperialism, we would have to think further about,
or at least make further comment about, Orwell's attitude toward imperialism. The syntax of the sentence would not permit us simply to assert
that Orwell's attitude existed.

Linguistic cue to use of focus:

The grammatical subject(s) of each clause in a piece of discourse.

Contrast. After focusing on some chunk of experience, we must, Pike
argues, perform certain operations in order to understand it. One of these,
contrast, entails knowing what an item (a word, a person, an object, a
feeling, etc.) is *not*, seeing how it differs from other items. Contrast is
operating when we make distinctions, when we have a sense of incongrui-
ty, or when we are aware of some disparity (between appearance and
reality, between the actual and the potential, between what we hope/
fear/wish to encounter and what we actually do encounter).

The *Beowulf* poet provides early illustrations of this process. Just after
Hrothgar has completed the mead hall Herot, the poet talks about the
monster Grendel:

> Then, when darkness had dropped, Grendel
> Went up to Herot, wondering what the warriors
> Would do in that hall when their drinking was done.
> He found them sprawled in sleep, suspecting
> *Nothing*, their dreams *undisturbed*. The monster's
> Thoughts were as quick as his greed or his claws:
> He slipped through the door and there in the
>   silence
> Snatched up thirty men, smashed them
> *Unknowing* in their beds and ran out with their
>   bodies,
> The blood dripping behind him, back
> To his lair, delighted with his night's
>   slaughter.

In this passage taken from the Burton Raffel translation, the poet makes
explicit the contrast between the unsuspecting warriors and the monster
who knows exactly what is about to take place. And the poet must assume
that the audience will feel the contrast between the monster's actions and
their own sense of honorable battle. To reinforce the contrast between

Grendel's actions and his audience's values, the poet notes that unlike ordinary people—indeed, even unlike ordinary monsters—Grendel is

> . . . . so set
> On murder that *no* crime could ever be enough,
> *No* savage assault quench his lust
> For evil.

Contrary to Anglo Saxon custom, the monster comes

> . . . . . . seeking *no* peace, offering
> *No* truce, accepting *no* settlement, *no* price
> In gold or land, and paying the living
> For one crime only with another.

Beowulf, too, is introduced through contrast. The hero is "*greater*/and
stronger than anyone else in this world."

Sometimes contrast is the means by which a writer tries to convey an
impression. When Huck Finn's Pap unexpectedly turns up in Huck's bed-
room at the Widow Douglas' house, Twain has Huck tell us that: "There
warn't no color in his face, where his face showed; it was white; *not* like
another Man's white, *but* a white to make a body sick, a white to make a
body's flesh crawl. . . ." Or contrast appears when people reflect upon
their own experiences. In *The South Goes North*, Robert Coles records
one young man's comments about his parents:

> My old man, he was *no* good. He drank all the time. You can
> have it; I like beer, *but I don't* drink the way he did. They found
> him dead in some alley. He was frozen to death, buried in snow.
> Can you beat that! And when they told her, my old lady, she *didn't*
> say anything. She *didn't* cry. She said she *didn't* even care. She told
> me my father really had been dead for five years, and the Lord was
> just too busy to notice and call for him. I thought she was fooling
> me, *but* she *wasn't*. My old lady, anything she says, she means.

When he thinks about his parents, the speaker is aware of several kinds of
contrasts: those between the father's actions and the speaker's values (the
father was "no good" because he drank constantly); between the speaker's actions and his father's (the young man drinks, too, but not as much as
his father did); between what his mother did and what she might have
done (she didn't say anything, didn't cry, didn't care when his father
died); and between what appeared to be the case and what actually was
so ("I thought she was fooling me but she wasn't."). In addition to these
contrasts, a reader is aware of further incongruities—chiefly that the
young man who condemns his alcoholic father is himself a heroin addict,
and hence his estimate of his own moral qualities is perhaps less reliable
than he might like to think.

Linguistic cues to use of contrast:

1 Connectors

or	but	instead
nor	however	though
else	nevertheless	although
lest	on the contrary	in spite
otherwise	on the other hand	despite
alternatively		

2 Comparative and Superlative Forms

more/most	less/least	-er/-est

3 Negative

no	without	none
not	nothing	

4 Negative Affixes

anti-	il-	un-
im-	dis-	non-
in-	less	a-
ir-		

5 Lexicon

Noun, verb, adjective, and adverb forms of such words as *contrast, paradox, distinction, difference,* and their synonyms.

Classification. Almost at the same time we think about the differences between X and Y, we have to think about their similarities. We have to see how people, actions, feelings, or ideas can be labeled or compared with other things. We have to think about what X reminds us of, what it has in common with other items in our experience. At worst, this can result in a simple-minded reductionism, which leads us to ignore the uniqueness of some phenomena and leaves us open to the charge that we are stereotyping. This danger notwithstanding, we can assume that one important way of knowing anything, especially something unfamiliar, is to know it in terms of something else.

One familiar form of classifying appears in the following passage from R. M. Lumiansky's translation of Chaucer's "The Miller's Tale." The Miller is describing one of the characters in his tale.

> The young wife was pretty, with a body *as* neat and graceful *as* a weasel. She wore a checked silk belt, and around her loins a flounced apron *as* white *as* fresh milk . . . her singing was *as* loud and lively *as* a swallow's sitting on a barn. In addition, she could skip about and play *like* any kid or calf following its mother. Her mouth was *as* sweet *as* honey or mead, or a pile of apples laid up in hay or heather. She was *as* skittish *as* a young colt, and tall and straight *as* a mast or wand. On her low collar she wore a brooch *as*

> broad as the boss on a shield. Her shoes were laced high on her legs. She *was* a primrose, a trillium, fit to grace the bed of any lord or to marry any good yeoman.

I do not cite this passage simply to give English teachers still another lesson in metaphor. I mean simply to suggest that metaphor (I use the term to include analogy and simile—any statement that asserts or implies that X is like Y or that X and Y share some common trait) is not simply a linguistic embellishment or a poetic refinement. The Miller's analogies reflect his own chauvinistic understanding of this young woman; when he thinks of her, he does so in these terms. As is often the case, his metaphors are an essential part of his understanding of his subject.

Another form of classification is suggested by the following group of letters (Simon 1962).

```
A B M N R S H I
C D O P T U J K
M N A B H I R S
O P C D J K T U
R S H I A B M N
T U J K C D O P
H I R S M N A B
J K T U O P C D
```

At first glance, this appears simply to be a random array of letters. But a closer look suggests that the letters are not random, they appear in patterns; certain relationships appear more than once. For example:

The point is, of course, that apparently complex phenomena can be simplified when we recognize that some patterns exist and that they are repeated. If we could not do this, we would have great trouble in thinking about—indeed, even in remembering—really complex experiences. The plot of *A Midsummer Night's Dream*, for example, is incredibly complicated. It requires that we keep track of several love stories that interweave confusingly and implausibly. Yet the play becomes reasonably coherent, almost simple, when we label recurrent motifs: for example, blindness, that caused by parental pride, by love, by egotism, or by magic potion.

Semanticists have pointed out how labeling influences thought. Saying "I am a loser" is quite different from saying "I lost the last two matches I played." And the difference is not, as S.I. Hayakawa notes, merely a matter of semantics (1972). The second statement comments only on the past. The first statement comments on the past *and* makes a prediction (often enough self-fulfilling) about the future.

The influence of labeling—sometimes a helpful influence, sometimes a harmful one—appears dramatically in people's efforts to solve problems. Consider, for example, students' work with the following problem, an extremely simple one when compared with the difficult social, moral, and personal problems we have to deal with most of the time. Two strings are suspended from a ceiling, perhaps ten or twelve feet apart. They are long enough so that, if one thinks imaginatively, a single person can manage to tie them together; but the strings are just short enough and just far enough apart so that one person cannot simply take hold of the end of one string and walk over and grasp the other. The problem is to bring the two strings together, receiving no help from anyone else and using only objects—usually a book, a pencil, and perhaps a chalkboard eraser—that have been left on a nearby table. One student who volunteered to try to solve this problem first tried to draw one string out to its full horizontal length and then reach to the other string. He couldn't quite reach far enough. He picked up the book on the table and used it as an extension of his reach; still no luck. He next picked up the pencil, clamped one end of it in the book, and tried to use the combination of book and pencil as a further extension of his reach.

The student solved the problem only when he reclassified, relabeled the pencil. Instead of thinking of it as a device to extend his reach, he thought of it as a weight, a pendulum weight. He then tied this weight to the end of one string and set it swinging back and forth. Next, he walked over, took the end of the other string, and walked back toward the first string, which swung neatly into his outstretched hand.

This sort of example, unfortunately, carries the danger that we will do our own labeling: "That's only an experiment, a trick, a clever gimmick."

Having thus labeled it, we can dismiss it and, ironically, provide a further example of the point I want to make: labeling is not just a matter of semantics; it is a fundamental part of our thinking.

Linguistic cues to use of classification:

1 Syntax

   Sentences in which a linking verb joins a subject with a predicate nominative. (My assumption here is that one of the noun phrases, either the subject or the predicate nominative, labels the other; that is, one of the noun phrases suggests a more general class, of which the other noun phrase is an instance or example.)

2 Use of Phrases

   for example   for instance
   an example   an instance

3 Lexicon

   Noun, verb, adjective, and adverb forms of such words as *similar, resemble,* and *class,* and their synonyms.

Not all the cues for contrast and classification are in themselves definitive. The significance of a cue may well be determined by the lexical context in which it appears. For example, accurate scoring could not be achieved simply by counting the individual cues in the following sentence: "They were more and more dissatisfied, but yet they were not interested in escaping from their predicament." Here, the linking verbs are not followed by predicate nominatives and thus do not indicate classification; the contrast cues "more," "more," and "dis-" suggest, when considered together, one reference to change rather than three references to contrast; and the phrase "but yet" is one lexical unit, suggesting one contrast, not two. Clearly, then, linguistic cues are simply a means of directing one's examination of a statement. One's sense of the meaning of a given statement must, finally, be the basis for determining what intellectual strategies have been used. It seems clear, however, that attention to linguistic cues can help judges agree as to what intellectual strategies are reflected in a written passage. When scorers were given linguistic cues in context, I found (Odell 1974) that scorers, working independently, could achieve 88% agreement in identifying the intellectual strategies an essayist was using.

Change. When Lady Macbeth first proposes that Macbeth murder Duncan, Macbeth hesitates, first citing the constraints of social and moral order, and then acknowledging his fear of failing at such a monstrous undertaking. But late in the play, after his second encounter with the witches, Macbeth resolves, "The very firstlings of my heart shall be/The firstlings of my hand." Murder—not only of those who pose an immediate threat to his ambitions but of children who may someday pose a threat—no longer gives him the slightest pause. Lady Macbeth, of course, undergoes equally extreme changes in exactly the opposite direction. By the end of the play, her "undaunted mettle" has dissolved. Completely undone by the enormity of her crime, she evokes only pity from the doctor and gentlewoman who observe her sleepwalking.

To understand either of these characters—indeed, Pike would contend, to understand anything—we must have a good sense of the nature and extent of the changes they undergo. For practical purposes, we assume that people, places, ideas remain essentially constant. In order to survive, we have to feel that things will be recognizable from one day to the next, that rules governing our existence will remain pretty much the same, that past experience will let us predict with some confidence what we may expect in the future. Yet we are amused, saddened, even horrified when someone denies the fact of change and carries that denial to its logical conclusion. A recent newspaper carried this caption underneath a picture of a famous star of western movies during the 1940s and 1950s:

> Roy and Dale!? Yup. Though Trigger is long since stuffed, the old straight shooter is riding hard . . . has a new movie, a restaurant chain, and maybe $40 million. "When my time comes, I want Dale to skin me and put me right up there on Trigger, just as if nothing had ever changed."

One hopes that the old straight shooter is being facetious. But serious or not, he helps make my point. Change is part of our experience; awareness of change is crucial to an understanding of experience.

Sometimes this awareness is painful. A policeman in Robert Coles' *The South Goes North* makes these comments (italics mine throughout):

> Do you see what has happened to this country in the last few years? The militants say they're going to *burn* their own neighborhoods down, and they're also going to *start coming* to our neighborhoods. Can you beat that? . . . I told my wife the other day that before we're out of this mess, they'll be setting more and more fires. There'll be fires everywhere in the ghetto, apart from when they riot, and they'll *start slipping* into our part of town. It'll mean a lot of work for me; no fooling.

The prospects of new social values, changes in his work, changes in the neighborhood, even in the country itself are as upsetting to him as a different sort of change was to Mark Twain when, serving as a "cub" pilot on a steamboat, he was trying to learn to navigate the Mississippi River.

> I went to work now to learn the shape of the river; and of all the eluding and ungraspable objects that ever I tried to get mind or hands on, that was the chief. I would fasten my eyes upon a sharp,

wooded point that projected far into the river some miles ahead of me, and go to laboriously photographing its shape upon my brain; and just as I was beginning to succeed to my satisfaction, we would draw up toward it and the exasperating thing would begin to *melt away* and *fold back* into the bank! If there had been a conspicuous dead tree standing upon the very point of the cape, I would find that tree inconspicuously *merged* into the general forest, and occupying the middle of a straight shore, when I got abreast of it! No prominent hill would stick to its shape long enough for me to make up my mind what its form really was, but it was as *dissolving* and *changeful* as if it had been a mountain of butter in the hottest corner of the tropics. Nothing ever had the same shape when I was coming down-stream that it had borne when I want up.

As he learned to deal with this sort of change, Twain had to reconcile himself to an even more profound change. After describing a really splendid sunset, he remarks:

I stood like one bewitched. I drank it in, in a speechless rapture. The world was new to me, and I had never seen anything like this at home. But as I have said, a day came when I began to *cease from noting* the glories and the charms which the moon and the sun and the twilight wrought upon the river's face; another day came when I *ceased* altogether *to note* them. Then, if that sunset scene had been repeated, I should have looked upon it without rapture, and should have commented upon it, inwardly, after this fashion: "This sun means that we are going to have wind to-morrow; that floating log means that the river is rising, small thanks to it. . . ."

Linguistic cues to reference to change:

1 Verb, noun, adjective, or adverb forms of the word *change* or a synonym for *change*.

2 Verb phrases which can be plausibly rewritten so as to include *become* (e.g., *realize-become aware*).

3 Verb phrases which include *began* (or a synonym) or *stop* (or a synonym) plus a verbal (e.g., "I began to cease from noticing. . . ").

Physical Context. As Beowulf lies waiting for Grendel to make his visit to Herot, the poet gives us a first look at Grendel—or rather at the surroundings in which Grendel characteristically appears.

Out from the marsh, from the foot of *misty*
Hills and *bogs*, bearing God's hatred,
Grendel came, hoping to kill
Anyone he could trap on this trip to high Herot
He moved quickly through the *cloudy night*,
Up from his *swampland*, sliding silently
Toward that gold-shining hall.

Later, Beowulf and others track Grendel's dam to her lair.

> Where *clumps of trees* bent across
> *Cold gray stones*, they came to a *dismal*
> *Wood*; below them was the *lake*, its *water*
> *Bloody* and *bubbling*.
> . . . .
> . . . They looked down at the *lake*, felt
> How its *heat* rose up, watched the *waves'*
> *Blood-stained swirling*. Their battle horns sounded,
> Then sounded again. Then they set down their weapons.
>   They could see the *water* crawling with snakes,
> *Fantastic serpents* swimming in the *boiling*
> *Lake*, and *sea beasts* lying on the *rocks*. . . .

The poet hardly needs to describe the monsters. He simply describes the physical context in which one typically finds them; our imaginations can do the rest.

Often enough, we see physical context used to influence our feelings. Cadillac ads locate the car in plush surroundings; President Nixon usually delivered televised speeches surrounded by an American flag, a bust of Lincoln, and a picture of his family. Perhaps the classic illustration of the importance of physical context appears in the movie *Blow-up*. Examining a picture he has taken of a park, a photographer discovers what appears to be a body lying in some bushes. He enlarges one section of the photograph, blowing it up until he has a picture of what is clearly a dead body. In the process of enlarging the picture, he has had to remove all physical context so that he can make the mysterious object large enough to identify. When his studio is burglarized, he is left with the one large picture of the dead body and a peculiar dilemma: he has proof that a murder has been committed but no way to prove to police that the body was ever located where he said it was. A picture of a body, removed from its physical surroundings, is almost meaningless to him and useless to the police.

Linguistic cues to physical context:

Nouns that refer to a geographical location (e.g., the name of a city, a geographic region, a point on a map), an object in a physical setting (e.g., a house or tree), a sensory property of a physical setting (e.g., the sound of wind in the trees).

Sequence. A ninth grader writes of a really frightening experience:

> Once, *when I was nine years old* I was upstairs in my house all alone watching T.V. It was about *10 o'clock*, my mom and dad said they would be back at *9 o'clock*. The monster movie that was on T.V. was "the man with a 1,000 eyes." The monster was a white glob with eyeballs all over him. It would go around killing people in dark alleys. This move was about the spookiest movie I had ever seen. I was watching a part *when* the movie was playing the spooky music *when* I knew something was going to happen,—like a man was going to get killed. *Then* I heard a creak from down stairs. . . .

Under most circumstances he probably wouldn't have worried about the noise; he might not even have heard it at all. But on this particular occasion, the noise becomes frighteningly significant because the student locates the noise in several sequences: 1) the sequence of his own life—he's old enough to be left alone at home but not old enough to be completely confident; 2) the sequence of his parents' actions—the noise occurs well after his parents were supposed to be home and, presumably, after he has had opportunity to become a little bit nervous anyhow; 3) the time sequence of the movie—the noise happens just when the "spooky music" is playing and just when he knows something horrifying is about to happen in the movie.

What is true for our understanding of a sound, of course, is also true for our understanding of/reaction to a person, an idea, an experience. Near the end of John Steinbeck's novel *Of Mice and Men*, George is repeating to Lennie the familiar story of the farm they will someday have.

> "Go on," said Lennie. "How's it gonna be? We gonna get a little place."
> "We'll have a cow," said George. "An' we'll have maybe a pig an' chickens . . . an' down the flat we'll have a . . . little piece alfalfa—"
> "For the rabbits," Lennie shouted.
> "For the rabbits," George repeated.
> "And I get to tend the rabbits."
> "An' you get to tend the rabbits."
> Lennie giggled with happiness. "An' live on the fatta the lan'.'"

Listening to the story we are aware, as Lennie is not, of its location in a time sequence. We know that Lennie has just killed Curly's wife, that even as George is talking Curly and a group of other pursuers are closing in, and that George is about to shoot Lennie. We also know something of why George acts as he does—he doesn't want Lennie to suffer at Curly's hands. We further realize that George is caught in an agonizing dilemma. If he doesn't kill Lennie, Curly will. If George does kill Lennie, he will also kill the dream that gives his life meaning, the one thing that distinguishes him from the other men.

Linguistic cues to reference to time sequence:

Adverbial elements indicating that something existed before, during, or after a moment in time. For example:

then	later	previously
when	meanwhile	earlier
next	subsequently	at that moment

Linguistic cues to reference to logical sequence:

1 Words implying a cause—effect relationship. For example:

because	since
therefore	consequently

2 The phrase *if . . . then . . . .*

Describing Student Writing

By identifying intellectual processes reflected in student writing, we can accomplish three slightly different but related objectives: making qualitative distinctions between pieces of writing done in the same mode and for the same audience; diagnosing writing problems; measuring growth in writing.

Making Qualitative Distinctions

Consider these two pieces; the first is by an eleventh grader, the second by a twelfth grader.

A Swingin' Dance

Yesterday, my boyfriend and I went to a big dance in Detroit. When we walked into the place, it was real noisy because everyone was talking and dancing. The dancing area was a lot bigger than most of the other ones I've seen, but the air was filled with smoke that would choke a horse. While looking around, my boyfriend noticed a few of his friends across the room, so we went over there, and he introduced them to me. They were the coolest guys. After talking a while with them, Fabian came up to me and asked me to dance. I just about died! I thought I was going to faint, but I pulled through. He's the most! I thought that my boyfriend was becoming a little jealous because of my reaction to Fabian, so I decided to go dance a dance or two with him. I danced off and on with him and some other boys the rest of the evening. On the way home I told him that I've never had such a riot at a dance before in my life. I don't know if that made him happy or sad.

Best of Pets

The bright beams peer ahead into the late dusk; I am driving home, Carlisle to Newcastle. Farm houses here along the road are far apart, and as I pass the few distant windows filled with light, I doubt that any inside are aware of my passing.

For a moment I ride the crest of a long hill; then, part way down, the lights play over a dim shape, alien to the rolling landscape. The car rolls to a stop beside it, the still figure of a well-groomed dog There is a little blood; only a wound on the jaw and the angle of the head indicate more or less than sleep. Likely less than an hour ago you left a nearby house, gone for a walk. They won't really be concerned till bedtime when you aren't there to curl up on the rug. Perhaps your owners should be told that you won't be coming home tonight, that you won't come running to the familiar call, or lie under the dinner table, or track mud into the house anymore . . Perhaps . . .

But what good would it do—And which house . . .? No, it seems best I go my way. You'll have to wait here till you're found. Until

then, for what they know, you're still out, soon to come home, and
life will be the same.

The car starts, the beams again clearing a path, and I drive on,
now for some reason slower than before, thoughts of my destina-
tion, and faint relief for other commitments just not able to . . block
. . the thought . . .

Each of these two pieces has certain problems. But, assuming that both
writers are trying to share an experience with an audience that doesn't
have firsthand knowledge of that experience, "Best of Pets" seems superi-
or to "A Swingin' Dance." Differences in word choice and syntax help
account for this value judgment. But even if I disregard these differences,
the latter essay still seems more perceptive, more carefully thought out;
the "Best of Pets" writer appears to have made more frequent and more
appropriate use of certain intellectual processes—*focus, reference to physical context, reference to sequence,* and *contrast.* Differences between
the two writers' use of *classification* and *reference to change* are small and
do not seem directly related to the essays' effectiveness or lack of effectiveness.

Focus.

"Best of Pets"	"A Swingin' Dance"
bright beams (2)	My boyfriend and I (we) (3)
I (6)	It (place)
farm houses	everyone
any	dancing area
lights	I (11)
the car (2)	air
wound on the jaw and angle	my boyfriend (he) (3)
of the head	They
You (dog) (6)	Fabian (he)
they (owners) (3)	that
life	
thoughts of destination	
and faint relief	

Both writers focus on *I*, as we might expect since they are writing about
their own experience. But the "Best of Pets" writer focuses on himself
only about 25% of the time; the "Swingin' Dance" writer focuses on herself
about 40% of the time. For certain purposes—especially if one were trying
to create a highly egocentric persona—this frequent focusing on oneself
seems appropriate. But the high proportion of clauses focused on *I* de-
creases the number of clauses that might focus on important aspects of
the experience the writer is trying to convey. In focusing less frequently

on himself, the "Best of Pets" writer is able to focus on, and make observations about, details (the dog, the farm houses, the car lights) that make the incident memorable. Moreover, the "Best of Pets" writer shifts focus interestingly. He not only focuses on the *car* but also on the car's *lights*, not only on the *dog* but also on *a wound on the* [dog's] *jaw* and *angle of the head*. By focusing not only on an object (*dog, car*) but on some specific facet of that object (*lights, wound*), he gives a sense of shifting attention, taking a careful look at what he's describing.

Physical Context.

"Best of Pets"	"A Swingin' Dance"
dusk	Detroit
Carlisle	the place (2)
Newcastle	the dancing area
farm houses	air
road	smoke
windows	room
crest of a long hill	
dim shape	
landscape	
still figure of a well-groomed dog	
house (3)	
rug	
dinner table	
mud	

At the beginning of each piece, the writers, in effect, set the scene for their experiences by referring to physical context. But the "Swingin' Dance" writer does so less effectively than does the writer of "Best of Pets." Of the seven references to physical context in "A Swingin' Dance," only the smoke-filled air and the large dancing area are distinctive features of the place she is describing. The other references to physical context (*Detroit, the place, the room*) are so general that they don't contribute anything to one's understanding of the writer's experience. Moreover, physical context has little to do with her feelings (she's more impressed with Fabian than with the dancing place) and it has nothing to do with the predicament she was in (her references to the dancing area don't heighten our understanding of her conflicting feelings about Fabian and her boyfriend). In "Best of Pets," however, all of the first nine references to physical context help establish the writer's sense of loneliness and isolation. Even if a bit sentimentalized, subsequent references to the dog's accustomed setting (*house, rug, table*) help readers understand why the dog was worth the writer's concern. Consequently, references to physical context help readers understand the writer's dilemma; he's in a physical context where a desirable course of action (locating the dog's owners) is not a feasible one.

Sequence.

"Best of Pets"	"A Swingin' Dance"
time sequence	time sequence
as I pass . . . I doubt	*yesterday* [we] went
For a moment I ride . . . crest	*When* we walked in . . . it was
less than an hour ago you left	noisy
won't . . . be concerned *till*	*While* looking around, [he]
bedtime	noticed
[become concerned] *when*	*After talking* . . . Fabian
you aren't there	came up
[not] coming home *tonight*	a dance *before*
track mud *anymore*	
wait here *till* you're found	causal sequence
Until then . . . you're still out	real noisy *because* everyone
soon to come home	was talking
drive on, *now* . . . slower	boyfriend [was] jealous
	because of my reaction
	jealous . . . *so* [therefore] I
	decided
	made him [caused him to be]
	happy or sad

In "A Swingin' Dance," three of the five references to time sequence locate actions (Fabian's appearance) and perceptions (noise of area, boyfriend's notice of friends) within the time sequence of the experience the writer is describing. Two of these refer to actions or perceptions occurring simultaneously (e.g., when we walked in, it was noisy). Moreover, all of the writer's cause-effect relationships occur within the time span of the evening. For example: Cause—boyfriend appeared to become jealous; Effect—she decided to dance with him. She does not suggest ways the present experience might have been influenced by previous events; nor does she speculate about how this experience might influence subsequent events, feelings, actions. By contrast, the writer of "Best of Pets" frequently speculates about events that precede or follow his finding the dead animal; eight of his eleven references to time sequence suggest events occurring in the past or in the future. Although his references to previous or subsequent events are not inherently good or bad, these references seem very appropriate here. They help communicate the significance he attributes to the animal and, consequently, help a reader understand why the writer feels so strongly about the experience.

Contrast.

"Best of Pets"

more or less than sleep
they *won't* be concerned
you *aren't* there
you *won't* be coming
    home
you *won't* come running
come running *or* lie . . . *or*
    track mud
But what good would it
    do
No, it seems . . .
it seems *best*
drive on . . . slow*er*
relief . . . *not* able to block
    the thought

"A Swingin' Dance"

[area was] *bigger than*
    most
[area was big] *but* air was
    filled with smoke
they were the *coolest*
    guys
I thought . . . *but* I pulled
    through
He's the *most*
I've *never* had such a riot
I *don't* know if that . . .
happy *or* sad

The "Best of Pets" writer dwells chiefly on two kinds of contrasts: 1) contrasts between a customary state of affairs (dog comes home sometime during the evening) and a new state of affairs; 2) contrasts between a course of action that seems right and desirable (trying to find the dog's owners) and a less attractive but more practical course of action (going on with his journey). These contrasts, combined with a final contrast between what he would like to do (block out the thought) and what he continues to do (dwell upon the experience), seem very clear. I understand what is different from/in conflict with what. In "Swingin' Dance," the contrasts are less clear. She contrasts the present experience with her own previous experiences (other dance areas she had seen were not as large as this one; she had had more of "a riot" at this dance than at others she had attended) and she contrasts people she meets (*the coolest, the most*) with other people whom she does not identify. As was the case with her repeatedly focusing on *I*, there are contexts (a conversation with or note to a close friend) in which her use of contrast is entirely appropriate. But, given her task of sharing an experience with someone who had no firsthand knowledge of that experience or of her previous experiences, her use of contrast seems less clear and less effective than does the "Best of Pets" writer's use of contrast.

Reference to Change.

" Best of Pets"	"A Swingin' Dance"
no references	I just about died boyfriend was becoming jealous

Although he talks about a thing that has undergone a change and implies that a change has taken place within himself (he has become preoccupied with the dilemma the dog presents), the writer of "Best of Pets" makes no explicit reference to change. The writer of "A Swingin' Dance" refers to a change within herself and infers that a change has occurred within her boyfriend; she makes no references to overt, physical changes in herself, other people, or objects.

Classification.

"Best of Pets"	"A Swingin' Dance"
life will be the *same*	They *were* the coolest guys.

The two writers make only negligible use of classification. Neither creates any analogies. Neither uses the subject/linking verb/predicate nominative structure to label people or objects in interesting or unusual ways.

In order to show how analysis of intellectual strategies lets us make distinctions between two roughly comparable pieces of writing, I have tried to give a fairly detailed example of how one might go about analyzing intellectual processes. In showing how this sort of analysis will let us diagnose student writing problems and measure students' growth in writing ability, my discussion can be more succinct.

Diagnosing Writing Problems

The following essay represents a classic problem in diagnosing and improving students' writing ability.

The College Freshman of 1975

The college freshman of 1975 has many doubts and questions. "Is college what I want?" "What courses are best for me?" These two questions are common with the college freshman and must be thought of seriously.

"Is college what I want?" Often the freshman is pushed into further and higher education. It may not be what he really wants. Every graduating high school senior must seriously ask himself this question and make the decision alone. The freshman will be more encouraged to succeed and achieve if he feels he has made the right decision.

> After he gets to college he asks himself, "What courses will I benefit from and which ones are required?" He often needs guidance from a counselor. If he chooses classes to his liking, he will be happier and try harder to achieve good grades. This has a good effect on the freshman and will encourage him to stay in school.
>
> The college freshman today is no different from a freshman fifty years ago. The fears are the same and the questions in his mind are puzzling. But if he has made the decision of furthering his education alone, then he has a far better chance of achieving his goal.

The great difficulty with this essay is that, in some respects, it is not a bad piece of writing. The organization is clear. And there are no errors in punctuation or spelling. But the paper is terribly dull. It gives no sense of the complexity, the drama, the interest of its subject. It reflects no real insight into the topic. One could, of course, tell the student this—let her know that she hasn't done her subject justice, that she needs to think more creatively, more profoundly, or one might resolve to devise future writing assignments that provide a clearer and more stimulating sense of audience and purpose. Each of these alternatives might be useful; I suspect neither is adequate. The care she took with the paper (her neat handwriting and careful proofreading of the draft she turned in) suggests that she's a reasonably conscientious, if uninspired, student. A change in audience and purpose for her writing would likely provide some inspiration and a reason to examine her subject more carefully and sensitively. But this change would not help her understand how she might carry out such an examination. If we want her to think better (more creatively, more profoundly, more analytically), we'll have to teach her how.

The process of improving her thinking will have to begin with our analysis of the intellectual processes she is currently using in her writing. We should notice, for example, the superficial, highly debatable classification in her last paragraph. (Are college freshmen today really the same as those of fifty years ago?) Notice, too, the simplistic hypothetical sequences she sets up. (Does she honestly believe that if classes are to students' liking they will inevitably be happier in college? Surely there are other influences that are equally important in determining students' happiness.) Finally, note that the subject of almost every clause is terribly general; she continually focuses on some mythical or composite creature (the college freshman of 1975) who has no individual personal reality for her or for her reader.

As we get a sense of how she's operating intellectually, we begin to see what we want her to learn to do. Her use of focus makes me think that she is not terribly observant; she apparently does not know how to look (literally, *look*) at real college freshmen and base her conclusions about them on her observation. Consequently, one important objective would be to have her learn to observe more closely by learning to shift focus. We could have her find examples of this process by watching television programs, noticing how the camera shifts focus, moving back to establish a physical setting, moving closer to capture the body language of a character, moving closer still to capture a small facial reaction. Or we could teach her this process by having her work with pictures (or, better still, with overhead transparencies made from magazine pictures). We could ask her to use large pieces of construction paper to block out everything in the picture except details (a person's smile, the expression in the person's eyes, a gesture) that say something important about the person in the picture. As she learns to shift focus from one important detail to another, we could encourage her to incorporate this process into her writing, making these details the subject of each clause and, hence, the topic about which the rest of the clause must assert something.

These suggestions for teaching are limited because they are derived from a diagnosis based on only one essay. To be genuinely useful and valid, a diagnosis should be based on several pieces of writing. But this brief discussion of one piece of writing should 1) show how an analysis of intellectual processes can supplement existing diagnostic procedures; 2) suggest ways this analysis might help a student write more effectively in the future.

Measuring Growth in Writing

In two other chapters in this book, Patrick Finn's work with computer analysis of word choice and Kellogg Hunt's study of syntax, we find powerful methods of measuring students' growth in two important aspects of writing. Analysis of intellectual processes lets us describe changes in another facet of students' writing—one that is not necessarily identified in Hunt's work or in Finn's. Syntax provides only a few cues to intellectual processes, and even those (e.g., coordinate conjunction cues to contrast, such as *but* and *however*; linking verb/predicate nominative cues to classification) need not be associated with lengthy or complex sentences. Similarly, lexical cues to a given operation (e.g., *not, change, when*) need not reflect a sophisticated vocabulary.

The following passages, a ninth grader's initial and revised drafts of a personal experience essay, will help explain how analysis of intellectual processes can be used in measuring students' growth in writing. The first piece was written prior to the beginning of a six-week course of study (Odell and Cohick 1975) in which students were introduced to intellectual processes described in this paper. The second piece, the revision, was done at the end of the six weeks.

One time when we went swimming my dad made me and my brother go off the high diving board. My brother went off and made it back to the side of the pool, but when I went off I did a bellyflop and almost drowned. My dad had to come in after me. I thought I was going to die because I couldn't breathe with all the water I swallowed in me.

When I was about eight years old my dad made me and my brother go off of this high diving board. When my brother got to the top I had butterflies because I knew I had to do it. I knew he would make it back out of the pool because he was a better swimmer than me. He jumped in feet first because it was too high for him to dive from. It took about 5 seconds for him to imerge. Then my dad made me do it. The treads on the steps were reassuring, but the railing was slippery, so I leaned in a little more than usual. When I got to the top I look at my dad and he waved me on. Then I look at my brother. He looked at me like it was really easy. I tried not to bounce as much as I could. I finally got up enough courage to jump. I don't think I heard anything around me because I was consintrating on the water. It looked a long ways down, but when I was on the bottom it wasn't that far. When I jumped I did a bellyflop and I was in so much pain I almost drowned. I could feel someone trying to keep my head above water, it was my dad. When we got out I was coughing because I swallowed some water. My dad had a "feeling sorry" laugh.

The revision explores the experience much more fully than does the original and reflects more effective use of several intellectual processes. In the revision, the ninth grader continues to focus on *I*; he even increases the proportion of clauses in which *I* is the subject. Yet he also increases the number of clauses focused on his father and brother, and each of these clauses contains relevant information that was not in the original. Moreover, the revision contains two clauses which focus on important parts of the physical context (*treads of steps* were reassuring; *railing* was slippery). These two references heighten one's sense of the writer's predicament.

The student's references to physical context, sequence, and contrast increase markedly in the revision. In the revised draft, he makes four times as many references to physical context, and at one point uses his failure to perceive physical surroundings as an indication of his internal state ("I don't think I heard anything around me because I was consintrating on the water."). In his second draft, the student locates eight actions (as opposed to one in the initial draft) within the time sequence of his narrative. He also cites five causal sequences, as opposed to one in the first draft. Finally, he uses a greater number of contrasts and more kinds of contrasts in the revision than in the original. In the first version, he notes one contrast between two actions (his brother's successful dive and his own "bellyflop") and one contrast between a normal and a peculiar state of affairs ("I couldn't breathe"). The second version contains six contrasts: one between his brother's swimming ability and his own ("He was a better swimmer than me."); one between two impressions (the reassurance provided by treads on the ladder steps, and the danger inherent in the slippery railing); one between an initial impression and a subsequent impression ("It looked a long ways down, but when I was on the bottom it wasn't that far."); and three contrasts between what he might have done and what he did do (tried not to bounce, leaned in more than usual, did not hear much while concentrating on the water below him).

With regard to the student's reference to change and his use of classification, there appears to be no important difference between the original and the revised essay. But the substantial changes in his use of other intellectual processes help account for the increased perceptiveness and effectiveness of the revision. On the basis of these two essays, admittedly an extremely limited writing sample, the student seems to be growing as a writer. Analysis of his use of intellectual strategies gives us another helpful way of monitoring that growth.

Questions Suggesting Further Study

Quantity and Quality

In each of the two pairs of essays discussed above, the quality of the essay seemed to be directly related to the number of intellectual processes reflected in the essay. Given information about the evidence and purpose for each pair of essays, classroom teachers and prospective teachers usually think that "Best of Pets" is better than "A Swingin' Dance" and that the ninth grader's revision is superior to his original draft. Since my analysis of intellectual processes would lead me to predict this sort of response, I wonder: Can we often make this sort of prediction with confidence? When trying to determine which of two comparable essays is the superior, can we assume that there is likely to be a strong connection between a reader's holistic judgment and the relative number of intellectual processes reflected in an essay?

Another sort of question arises from my analysis of the ninth grader's writing. As I suggested, the ninth grader's revised essay about a frightening experience contains many more contrasts than does the original paper. But the revision also contains more different *kinds* of contrasts than does the original. In the revision, the writer notes contrasts between two concurrent impressions, between an earlier impression and a subsequent impression, and between a potential action and the way he actually did behave. Consequently, I wonder: Can we identify subcategories for each intellectual process that will let us make finer discriminations between two pieces of writing?

Relation to Other Descriptive Procedures

Given the usefulness of descriptive procedures Finn and Hunt have developed, it seems important to ask several questions: Can the procedures I've discussed complement theirs? Would a really thorough description and measurement of growth in writing need to include information about word choice, syntax, and intellectual processes? Would such a description help us make more adequate diagnoses or formative evaluations of students' writing? Would instruction based on such diagnosis have a greater effect on students' writing than instruction based on a more limited diagnosis?

Developmental Considerations

In Hunt's work, we have a comprehensive view of the development of syntactic fluency. Can we find equally significant developmental qualities in people's use of intellectual processes? Almost certainly anyone who can make a coherent statement can use at least some of the intellectual processes I've described. But do people at different age levels use different intellectual processes? Do they use different subcategories of intellectual processes? For example, do seventeen year olds observe different kinds of contrasts than do nine year olds? If so, can we obtain, as Hunt did for syntax, a sense of what intellectual processes are possible for or likely to occur at a given age? If so, could this information improve our teaching and measurement of composition?

Conclusion

As the preceding section suggests, the effort to solve one problem—that of finding ways to describe writers' use of certain intellectual processes— leads to new problems. Moreover, as we answer the kinds of questions I've tried to raise, we will likely encounter new questions which make still further demands on our resourcefulness in describing and measuring growth in writing. As we meet these demands, it seems almost certain that we will make important advances in measurement, in rhetorical theory, and in the teaching of writing. More sophisticated, comprehensive descriptions of written products should lead us to reexamine our basic assumptions about written products and the process of writing. And this combination of improved theory and descriptive procedures seems to offer our best hope of achieving one important goal of measurement and evaluation: making statements that describe accurately and usefully students' present writing and that have clear implications for students' subsequent writing.

Bibliography

Hayakawa, S. I. *Language in Thought and Action*. 3d ed. New York: Harcourt Brace Jovanovich, 1972.

Odell, L. "Piaget, Problem-Solving, and Freshman Composition." *College Composition and Communication* 24 (1973): 36–42.

———. "Measuring the Effect of Instruction in Pre-writing." *Research in the Teaching of English* 8 (1974):228–40.

Odell, L., and Cohick, J. "You Mean, Write It Over in Ink?" *English Journal* 64 (December 1975):48–53.

Pike, K. L. "A Linguistic Contribution to Composition." *College Composition and Communication* 15 (1964a):82–88.

———. "Beyond the Sentence." *College Composition and Communication* 15 (1964b):129–35.

Rohman, D. G., and Wlecke, A. O. *Pre-writing: The Construction and Application of Models to Concept Formation in Writing*. Cooperative Research Project, no. 2174. 1964, Michigan State University, Office of Education, U.S. Department of Health, Education and Welfare.

Simon, H. A. "The Architecture of Complexity." *Proceedings of the American Philosophical Society* 106 (1962):467–82.

Steinmann, M. "Speech-Act Theory and Writing." Unpublished paper presented at the Buffalo Conference on Researching Composing, Buffalo, 1975.

Young, R. E.; Becker, A. L.; and Pike, K. L. *Rhetoric: Discovery and Change*. New York: Harcourt Brace Jovanovich, 1970.

Young, R. E., and Koen, F. M. *The Tagmemic Discovery Procedure: An Evaluation of Its Uses in the Teaching of Rhetoric*. Ann Arbor, Mich.: University of Michigan. National Endowment for the Humanities Grant no. EO 5238-71-116, 1973.

The preceding chapters suggest procedures which students might be taught to use in examining their own and their classmates' writing. But the following article is the only one to give direct attention to two basic questions: Should we engage students in the process of describing and measuring growth in writing? If so, how do we go about it? In response to these questions, Beaven gives a careful analysis of the rationale for and advantages/disadvantages of students' participation in the process of evaluation. Further, Beaven describes three basic ways students might be involved in this process. Indirectly, this article speaks to concerns—such as diagnosis and summative or formative evaluation—treated in other articles. The unique contribution of this article is that it asks us to reconsider students' relation to the evaluation process and to share with students some of the responsibility for describing and measuring their own growth in writing.

INDIVIDUALIZED GOAL SETTING, SELF-EVALUATION, AND PEER EVALUATION

Mary H. Beaven

Introduction

When one looks for research that might help classroom teachers evaluate student writing more effectively, not much is available that seems immediately applicable. In 1963 Braddock, Lloyd-Jones, and Schoer wrote, "Research has so far given no clear indications of the most efficacious way to mark papers." Twelve years later, in 1975, Jerabek and Dieterich, in their review of research on the evaluation of student writing, wrote: "Insufficient research has been done on the subject, a fact which accounts for much of our ignorance. But the little research that has been done is too seldom translated into classroom practices."

However, as the other chapters in this book indicate, research is going on, and important strides are being made in identifying various kinds of discourse, analyzing the composing process, and designing ways to describe and evaluate the stages of the process. Researchers are developing and refining methods to evaluate writing for the National Assessment of Educational Progress, and Educational Testing Services is continuing its explorations. At colleges and universities, professors and their graduate students are devising ways to help classroom teachers look at writing and respond to it.

As I have worked with English teachers and as they have experimented and reported on their work with formative evaluation procedures in their classrooms, we have evolved three approaches for responding to student writing: individualized goal setting, self-evaluation, and peer evaluation. In these three procedures, the individual student, not the researcher or the teacher, assumes a prominent role.

As the student becomes increasingly adept at evaluating writing, he or she will be able to use many ways of describing/responding/evaluating, some of which are outlined in the other chapters of this book. For example, children in elementary school can begin to identify the thinking processes of comparing, contrasting, classifying, and sequencing as described by Odell in this book and then to experiment with these strategies in their own writing. They can also learn to identify T-units and embeddings and to combine sentences as they write. They can analyze the level of their vocabulary, use some of the rating scales, and begin to view writing holistically. Older students can refine these abilities and go on to devise writing assignments that elicit a specific type of discourse and to evaluate the results with the guidelines Lloyd-Jones suggests in his chapter.

In the three methods of describing/responding/evaluating to be presented in this chapter, the teacher serves as a resource person or facilitator, and the individual student assumes increasingly greater responsibility: judging, making decisions, and then acting accordingly.

Basic Assumptions

Six assumptions underlie the three approaches to formative evaluation. These assumptions derive from two basic premises.

1 Growth in writing is a highly individualistic process.
2 Many procedures designed to foster personality growth also relate to growth in writing.

The first assumption is that, although many research studies dealing with the efficacy of various methods of instruction have failed to show significant improvement in writing, *improvement may occur over a much longer period of time than the six-, ten-, or even fifteen-week periods which teachers and researchers usually allow. Growth in writing occurs slowly.*

This assumption is reinforced by those who have studied syntactical development and found that linguistic ability develops slowly. For instance, linguists and others studying oral language development in early childhood have shown that children, once they begin using plural forms of nouns, may take from eight to nineteen or twenty months to achieve mastery (Cazden 1972, pp. 41-47). Kellogg Hunt has found it reasonable to look for changes in written syntactical structures at two- and four-year intervals.

The second assumption is that *through their evaluatory comments and symbols teachers help to create an environment for writing.* Some negative comments may teach students that descriptions of certain topics, feelings, values, perceptions, etc., are taboo. For example, when I was in grade school, one of my papers was returned with this comment: "I cannot grade thoughts such as these. You must write about something nice or pretty." Furthermore, if teachers pounce on mechanical and sentence errors, decorating a paper with red marks, students may begin to believe that they have nothing acceptable to communicate.

This assumption is supported by research indicating that the creation of a climate of trust is essential. Linguists interested in oral language development in early childhood have shown that adult responses to children's verbalization affect motivation to talk, amount of speech, and so on. Adults who respond to the content and ideas of the child and carry on a "conversation," regardless of the child's grammar or syntax, are reinforcing positive language development, the motivation to talk, the desire to have "something to say," and the ability to experiment with language, stretching it to accommodate an expressive need (Cazden 1972). In one study on writing, done over a ten-week period, the results showed that students who received only positive commentary on their papers developed a more positive attitude toward writing than those receiving negative commentary (Stevens 1973).

My next two assumptions are related, since they both refer to characteristics found in people who have an achievement syndrome, "a cluster of traits that relate to the way a person goes about attaining his goals." In continuing the above description of such a person, deCharms (1968, p. 232) has written:

> Research has given us a picture of a man with high achievement motivation. He is the man who takes moderate risks, attains his goals through energetic and novel instrumental activity, likes to take individual responsibility and to know the results of his actions and plans, and organizes his life and is concerned about the use of his time.

Risk-taking, trying new behaviors as one writes, and stretching one's use of language and toying with it are important for growth in writing. Rogers (1962) describes the fully-functioning person as one who prefers growth to safety, seeking opportunities for "play" with perceptions, ideas, emotions, modes of expression, etc. According to Maslow (1962 and 1971), risk-taking is a trait of self-actualizing people, a trait which can be developed as teachers provide the necessary environment, opportunities, and interpersonal support. Maslow (1971) states that through participation in the creative arts people develop risk-taking abilities, becoming more fully-functioning; he argues that education should be centered on participation in creative expression in all the arts, writing included.

Goal setting is also an important process in the development of student writers. In their work on achievement motivation, McClelland et al.

(1953) illustrate how goal setting helps to create conditions necessary for improvement or achievement. Apparently, goals need to be concrete and within reach, and students need to see the results of their actions. The implication for teachers is that students should work toward a limited number of goals at a time and that progress toward specified goals should be recorded.

A fifth assumption is that *writing improvement does not occur in isolation*. Merely assigning themes and arranging for some sort of evaluation prove insufficient, because writing is related to speaking, listening, reading, and all the other avenues of communication available for processing information. Prewriting activities, revisions, sensory awareness experiences, responses to literature, development of sensitivity to self and others—these and many other experiences, both in and out of the English classroom, affect a student's growth in writing.

The final assumption is that *we have a reasonably clear understanding of procedures that will permit effective formative evaluation*. Charles Cooper (1975, p. 113) writes:

> I think a better scheme for writing instruction . . . is one concerned with *diagnosing* what students are able to do and what problems they are having; *arranging for writing often* in many modes; *correcting usage and syntactical and rhetorical deficiencies organically* by working with the students' own writing and not by preteaching rules; *giving feedback and encouragement*, as each of the students' efforts moves them toward better control of a particular mode of writing; and finally *assessing how much growth students have shown* during the course, without comparing them invidiously to each other and without expecting "mastery." The emphasis in this scheme is on diagnosis, on formative response and evaluation to enhance the complex and highly individualistic process. . . .

These six assumptions are important and have influenced the three evaluative procedures I will be describing.

Developing a Climate of Trust for Writing

As a prerequisite to developing writers, teachers must develop a climate of trust. Student writers need to develop trust in their own powers to communicate through writing; to explore feelings, ideas, and perceptions through writing; and to find security in transactions with their audience of teachers, peers, or others.

As the teachers I have worked with have looked for ways to create trust through their evaluatory comments, two authors have influenced them most. Virginia Axline (1964) and Carl Rogers (1954 [with R. F. Dymond] and 1961) have developed ways of responding that teachers have successfully adapted to student writing. The kinds of comments presented below seem to be effective in creating a climate of trust.

1 A teacher may ask for more information: "I'd like to know more about this." "What did the other kids do?" "Have you seen _____ _____ on Channel 26 on Tuesday nights?" "Do you think there is a relation between this idea and the one John was talking about yesterday in class?"

2 A teacher may mirror, reflect, or rephrase the student's ideas, perceptions, or feelings: "You sound angry here." "You really do find school boring." "You want to be both an artist and businessman."

3 A teacher may share with the student times when he or she felt, thought, or behaved in a similar fashion: "I had problems with my parents, too. They insisted I be home by 11:00 p.m. on weekends!" "I still am lonely—perhaps all people feel that way at times."

As teachers have consistently and exclusively used these forms of commentary, they have found that the dull, lifeless prose Ken Macrorie (1970) labels "Engfish" tends to decrease; students shed depersonalizing modes of expression, writing their own thoughts and feelings, becoming more authentic, and developing individual voices. In addition, students who are scared of writing begin to increase the length of their efforts, and those puny six-to ten lines of timid prose become longer and more forceful.

Several of my graduate students used these methods with their classes this fall. The following remarks are typical of their reactions:

> My kids spontaneously are writing pages in response to my questions—all because I asked them a personal question.

> I never knew my students had so much going on in their lives. I seem to be following 130 different soap operas just because I've changed my ways of responding.

Not only do these responses serve to combat Engfish, to motivate students to write more, and to inspire more authentic writing, they also serve as reinforcement. Comments such as "No one else but you could have written it that way," and "Your figure of speech is just right, I think," indicate effective elements of writing and help students develop critical abilities. Furthermore, comments may also reinforce positive values. For example, in a theme describing happiness almost entirely in terms of material possessions, a student had one sentence mentioning happiness as "having a wife and children to love and friends to share the years." His teacher reinforced that value by writing, "My family and friends seem to give my life its purpose and meaning." She had no need to criticize or moralize; the statement she made underscored a value seemingly lost among cars, clothes, travel, and houses. In addition, such comments enable teachers to ask the kinds of value clarification questions suggested by

Raths, Harmin, and Simon (1966). For example, "Is it more important to you to have a family and friends or to have three fantastic homes?"

Whether papers are evaluated through individualized goal setting, self-evaluation, or peer evaluation, the three kinds of commentary suggested above are appropriate and necessary to create a climate of trust.

Individualized Goal Setting

Description

Individualized goal setting is carried out by the teacher, utilizing the kinds of comment detailed in the previous section. Guidelines for individualized goal setting follow.

1 Decide how you are going to respond: written comments, tape-recorded comments, a rating scale, or personal conference. (Coleman [1972] compared marginal and terminal written commentary with audio-taped remarks, finding that black students and students with low pretest scores responded better to the taped comments than the white students. Classes using taped responses developed a more positive attitude toward writing. Bata [1972] discovered no significant differences among three classes of junior college freshman papers evaluated in three different ways [marginal comments vs. terminal comments vs. a mixture]. Stanton [1973] compared groups receiving feedback in the form of written commentary, a checklist, teacher instruction, and questions and feedback, finding no significant differences although a checklist helped teachers be more reliable. Maize [1952] discovered that, when an instructor worked with college-level freshmen as they wrote in class and met in peer groups, evaluation was more effective than when an instructor corrected papers outside class. Wormsbecker's [1955] research showed no significant differences among the writing samples collected from three different groups who received either overall improvement suggestions, a split grade [form over content], or a single suggestion for improvement.)

2 Read the paper and, where the motivation is genuine and spontaneous, use commentary for developing a trusting environment.

3 When you have read the paper, offer one positive comment, either general or specific.

4 Establish a goal for the student to work toward, stating it in a positive way: not, "Your paper is a disaster because it lacks organization;" but, "For your next paper write as vehemently, but after you

have sounded off, read your draft and revise, putting all your thoughts on one idea in the same paragraph." (Some students may have more than one goal.) Encourage students to experiment and take risks.

5   Evaluate the student's next paper according to the goal(s) previously prescribed. Do not prescribe additional goals until the student is able to handle ones already given. (Stevens [1973], in a ten-week period, discovered no significant differences between a group that received only negative comments and one that received only positive remarks although students receiving positive comments had more positive attitudes toward writing. Groff [1975], in his review of research concerning the evaluation of younger children's writing, found that negative criticism seemed to have a positive effect, particularly on mechanics. Buxton [1958] presented some evidence that writing of college freshmen improved more when it was thoroughly marked than when a few general suggestions were offered. Schroeder [1973] found that corrective feedback produced more writing improvement than only positive feedback in composition work with fourth graders. Arnold's study [1964] compared students writing frequently with little evaluation with others receiving extensive commentary with still others who received a mixture; no significant differences. Although mixed, research does seem to indicate that setting goals for improvement is beneficial.)

6   Every three to four weeks, depending on how much writing is done, have students revise a paper for a more thorough evaluation. (Underwood [1968] found that grades used with marginal comments improved mechanics, but content improved without grades or marginal comments when revisions were required.)

Rationale

Because the teacher knows each student, goals may be tailored, in a diagnostic-prescriptive fashion, to meet individual needs. A goal may be as specific as "Spell *tomorrow, occasion,* and *recommend* correctly from now on," or as general as "Develop your own voice; your writing should sound as if you and no one else were writing." Students feel a sense of self-worth and esteem as they progress at their own speed in their own idiosyncratic fashion, with direction when needed. By limiting attention to a few goals at a time, the student is better able to concentrate on the content of the communication while the teacher does not have to spend an inordinate amount of time on each paper.

Advantages and Disadvantages

Individualized goal setting, of the three approaches the most effective in creating a climate of trust, proves most advantageous at the beginning of the school year when students and teacher are new to each other. It provides an opportunity for a teacher to become acquainted with students, to develop an accepting atmosphere, and to assess writing strengths and weaknesses. Many teachers and students feel most comfortable with the highly-structured individualized goal setting because the teacher stays in control, diagnosing and prescribing work for individual students. Another advantage of individualized goal setting results from tapping the knowledge, awareness, and writing experience of the teacher. There are times when a teacher's perceptions and suggestions may prove fruitful and economical as a student works through a revision or toward specific goals on a week-to-week basis.

On the other hand, there is at least one disadvantage to individualized goal setting. When a teacher is the exclusive audience for writing, students become dependent upon the teacher, an authoritarian figure who bestows approval or disapproval. Every time I have a new group of graduate students, many of whom have become addicted to having their writing analyzed and labeled by some "expert," we must break that addiction. Writers must realize how their writing affects peers and learn to depend more upon their own powers of judgment.

Teachers who have experimented with the three approaches to evaluation have found individualized goal setting most helpful with those students who require more direction and guidance, at the beginning of the year, and at times when those engaged in peer or self-evaluation seem to need help in perceiving new possibilities for experimentation.

Self-Evaluation

Description

In self-evaluation, students comment on their own writing and establish their own goals for risk-taking and improvement. Many teachers have found this sort of procedure helpful to use early in the school year because it leads the student toward greater self-reliance and independence. Early in the term, students evaluate their own papers and then turn them in for a modified individualized goal setting evaluation, with the teacher commenting upon the evaluation written by the student.

The following questions form the basis for self-evaluation procedures throughout the year:

1 How much time did you spend on this paper?
2 (After the first evaluation) What did you try to improve, or experiment with, on this paper? How successful were you? If you have questions about what you were trying to do, what are they?
3 What are the strengths of your paper? Place a squiggly line beside those passages you feel are very good.
4 What are the weaknesses, if any, of your paper? Place an X beside passages you would like your teacher to correct or revise. Place an X over any punctuation, spelling, usage, etc., where you need help or clarification.
5 What one thing will you do to improve your next piece of writing? Or what kind of experimentation in writing would you like to try? If you would like some information related to what you want to do, write down your questions.
6 (Optional) What grade would you give yourself on this composition? Justify it.

Because students tire of the same questions, teachers need to vary them from week to week, adding questions related to the current work of the class.

The importance of self-evaluation may be revealed through an analysis of the questions themselves and of the relations between the questions and the assumptions presented at the beginning of this chapter.

By asking a student to reveal the amount of time spent on a composition, the teacher is alluding to the fact that often writing is a long, complex, and agonizing process, one that sometimes does not flow rapidly but stumbles about awkwardly. To make this question more meaningful, the teacher can share in class some of the letters or descriptions of the creative process as put forth by established writers. Flaubert, Melville, Miller (1964), and others have described their struggles to say something "right"; Nin (1968), Miller, Forster, Lowes, and others talk about the unconscious prewriting that occurs; and still others portray the times when their writing flowed rapidly in a mystical sort of way. As students become more aware of the creative process, this particular question can be changed to ask for information about their processes in writing a particular composition. Soon, revealing information comes forth:

> I read two books on the subject, becoming very excited, but when I started writing, I didn't know how to start. I must have ripped up twenty sheets with various introductory paragraphs. Next I tried outlining—four outlines later I was still dissatisfied. So, because the time was getting short and I had already spent thirty-five hours on this damned paper, I began writing, wrote for six hours, and typed it up. The stuff goes in circles and never gets anywhere. I am disappointed. It is a flop—a complete disaster.

> I thought a lot about my paper, even dreamed about it one night.
> When I sat down to write it early this morning, it was all there. My
> mind must have been working on it, organizing it, during the week.
> Everything came out all right, and I am proud of the paper—
> except that I feel a little guilty because the actual writing went as
> smoothly and rapidly and I know others in the class spent hours.

The teacher, as this kind of information is shared, can help students
deal with their own creative processes, helping them to recognize that at
times all writers write in circles. And as students analyze their own creative processes and compare them with others, they begin to recognize
various strategies they might try.

The third question, asking a student to identify the strengths of his or
her paper, is important for three reasons. First, according to Jourad
(1963), Maslow (1962 and 1971), Rogers (1954 [with R. F. Dymond] and
1961), and others, most people have difficulty praising themselves and
accepting praise from others. "I'm O.K." is hard to say and "You're O.K."
is difficult to accept. These difficulties have developed through conditioning; asking students to identify strengths of their papers is one way to
combat this cultural conditioning. Second, many students have never considered the possibility that there *could* be something good about their
writing; for years they have been churning out the stuff because they were
obliged to do so. To have to point out something of which they are proud
motivates students to write from a different perspective. In my experience and in that of my fellow teachers, we have found that this one question motivates students to work on passages until they are "just right." The
third reason for the question is that writers must eventually become independent, able to identify passages that gracefully communicate meaning
and intention; writers must become their own editors and form their own
aesthetic judgments.

The fourth question also refers to the editorial process and to aesthetic
judgment because it asks students to locate weak passages. By asking students to do this, teachers indicate that they expect students to have problems in writing; it is acceptable to have them. And when a student indicates where he or she wants help and red-pen marks, he or she remains in
control of the evaluation process because red marks are applied only
upon invitation. As Smith (1975) points out, comprehension and learning
occur when the students' expressed questions and needs are addressed.

Self-evaluation is also helpful during various stages of revision. Beach
(1976) asked twenty-six preservice English teachers to write a draft, tape-
record their self-evaluations, revise, tape-record, revise and tape-record
until they were satisfied. By analyzing their taped comments and the
changes they made, he found that fifteen of these teachers were nonrevisers, concentrating on details, labeling them (frag, awk, etc.), and making

superficial changes as they were "smoothing out," "polishing," and "tying together." The extensive revisers attained an aesthetic distance the nonrevisers lacked, for they looked at their writing in holistic, general ways, seeing how the parts fit together as they developed a sense of an overall structure. Once they saw a structure emerge, they worked with their material until the revision matched the conceptual, structural vision.

When we ask students to request help where needed, we discover students' perceptions of their writing. Students who request help only for mechanical errors, not noticing a need for restructuring, may need help in revision strategies; they may not perceive the need to reconceptualize the structure and to relate the parts to the whole.

The fifth question is also designed to give a student more control over his or her own progress in writing. Asking a student to establish a goal for experimentation or improvement strengthens risk-taking capacities, decision-making capabilities, and goal-setting processes. Furthermore, because the writing process is so complex, perhaps the student knows best where he or she needs to improve or experiment (conditions under which the writing is done; prewriting strategies; original drafts; revision tactics; kinds of discourse; styles). One student, working full time in addition to attending high school and living in a large family, believed that her biggest problem was that she could find no time or place to be alone to think and prepare a first draft. Several weeks of experimentation helped: she woke up at 3:00 a.m., locked herself in the bathroom, and wrote from 3:00-5:00 a.m. In another instance, a college student, psychologically unable to write poetry or short stories, revealed that unless she stuck to critical, expository essays, painful memories of three deaths from cancer in her family surfaced and paralyzed her. Once she realized she was in a climate of trust and acceptance, she set up goals: to write about those deaths and deal with the issues. About two months later she was writing freely in a variety of modes. Only when a student is free to decide upon his or her own goals for improvement or experimentation, will he or she be able to explore those elements which impede progress—elements which a teacher or peers may know nothing about.

Obviously related to the fourth and fifth questions, the second question places the responsibility upon the student to follow through on the decisions made on the last self-evaluation. Again, researchers in achievement motivation emphasize the importance of goal setting and evaluation:

> The more an individual commits himself to achieving concrete goals in life related to the newly formed motive, the more the motive is likely to influence his future thoughts and actions.
>
> The more an individual keeps a record of his progress toward achieving goals to which he is committed, the more the newly formed motive is likely to influence his future thoughts and actions.

> Changes in motives are more likely to occur in an interpersonal
> atmosphere in which the individual feels warmly but honestly sup-
> ported and respected by others as a person capable of guiding and
> directing his own future behavior. . . .
>
> Changes in motives are more likely to occur the more the setting
> dramatizes the importance of self study. . . . (deCharms 1968)

Question six, optional, asks the student to place a grade upon the paper.
If a school system insists that grades be given, I feel that it is oppressive
for teachers to label and grade students and their work; students should
have the power to grade and label themselves in such a way that they
have to sift through a number of factors, balance them, and decide upon a
grade. In my experience I find that my assessment and that of the students
correspond in 90% of the cases, and the 10% discrepancy provides a start-
ing point for discussion in individual conferences.

Teachers and students have found rating scales helpful in providing
structure for self-evaluation. (Refer to Charles Cooper's chapter for a discussion of some of the available scales; some of the ideas presented in the
other chapters may also be adapted and introduced as self-evaluation
strategies.)

Rationale

Self-evaluation procedures help students assume responsibility for assessing their writing. As one teacher said, "For the first time my students
are seeing beyond the stage of just writing a paper, handing it in, and
forgetting about it. They are learning to look at their papers through critical eyes, becoming more aware of areas in which they can improve their
writing on their own." Perhaps self-evaluation procedures are essential for
helping students become their own editors, knowing what needs revision
and knowing how to go about that revision. Such procedures also encourage students to formulate questions, helping the teacher to know what is
needed when it is needed.

Not only is this approach educationally sound, but it also relates to the
development of a fully-functioning personality. Rogers (1954 [with R. F.
Dymond], 1961, and 1962) states that one of the three characteristics of a
creative personality is an inner locus of evaluation, and students need
many opportunities in school to develop that inner locus. In their work
with achievement motivation, McClelland et al. (1953), finding that individualized goal setting and self-evaluation bring about achievement, have
developed theoretical frameworks from which others, such as Otto (1968),
Alschuler (1973), and Alschuler, Tabor, and McIntyre (1970), have
evolved specific manuals and training programs based upon goal setting

and self-evaluation. Fromm (1947 and 1966) illustrates how people become dependent upon authority figures, failing to outgrow their need for them; he points out clearly that people need to become more responsible for charting their own goals and evaluating their own efforts. Ekstein and Motto (1969) contend that children initially work to please their teachers; yet to mature as learners, they must begin to decide what they are going to learn, how to go about that learning process, and how to evaluate their own progress; motivation and evaluation must become internalized. Self-assertion training programs relate to this need for people to become self-evaluative and then to act in accord with their own evaluations. As one reads the works of educational and psychological researchers, theorists, and practitioners, the cry for self-evaluation procedures sounds forth like a clarion.

Advantages and Disadvantages

Unlike peer evaluation, self-evaluation need not consume large amounts of class time; unlike individualized goal setting, self-evaluation need not consume the teacher's after-school hours. Self-evaluation can occur in class within five to ten minutes, although, if so desired, it can be used in conjunction with one of the other modes of evaluation.

Of all three forms of evaluation, self-evaluation allows students the most freedom to decide their individual courses of action, developing editing skills in the process. It promotes self-reliance, independence, autonomy, and creativity.

The primary disadvantage results from cultural mores and conditioning. Teachers are supposed to be authoritarian experts while students, supposedly knowing little, depend upon the mandates of those in power. And, indeed, teachers tend to become uncomfortable when they forego some of their power, control, and authority; they feel as if they are "not doing their job," "slacking their efforts," "not giving students what they deserve and what taxes are paid for." Sometimes if only self-evaluation procedures are used for more than two weeks, students begin to experience existential anxiety, feeling uncomfortable with freedom and wanting to escape from it. They tend to panic, begging teachers to assume the responsibility and give them grades. A number of parents, in one case, even called the school to demand that teachers not abdicate their responsibility.

Consequently, if a teacher wants to make *extensive* use of self-evaluation procedures, he or she needs to have the interpersonal skills or counseling techniques to work through these conflicts and to help students and parents deal with the anxiety generated. In some cases, a guidance counselor has worked with teachers and students until all are comfortable. However, it should be noted that, used intermittently or simultaneously with other evaluation procedures, self-evaluation causes few, if any, problems. Problems emerge only when this approach is used extensively by itself.

Peer Evaluation

Description

The third approach to evaluation involves peers who meet in small support groups to respond to each other's writing. However, before peer evaluation begins, a climate for sharing must be developed, during which time individualized goal setting and self-evaluation work well. The interpersonal skills needed for peer evaluation can also be developed at this time. A suggested procedure follows.

1 First stage. Students work in pairs on tasks that take fifteen to twenty minutes to complete. (These tasks do not have to be related to writing or even English.) "Work with someone you do not know" and "Work with someone you have not worked with before" are criteria for selection of partners.

2 Second stage. Students work in groups of four on tasks of fifteen to twenty minutes. Groups change with each task. A group of students working in front of the rest of the class can be used to model and shape desired group behavior. Roles (recorder, discussion leader, etc.) may be assigned. When all students seem accepted in these groups, the class progresses to the next stage.

3 Third stage. The teacher assigns students to groups for sustained projects. Evaluation procedures may be used to focus on group dynamics and interpersonal skills.

4 Fourth stage. Students select their own groups for sustained projects or support.

5 Whenever necessary or appropriate, a class may return to a prior form of group work.

Highly-structured forms (rating scales) may be used as soon as students are comfortable in the first stage; structure is also needed in the second stage. However, the desired growth in writing seems to occur when students work with the same group for an extended period and when there is less structure. (For a thorough discussion of group processes, refer to Yalom 1975. For a more practical approach, refer to Stanford and Stanford 1969, or Sax and Hollander 1972.)

During peer evaluation, teachers need to provide many opportunities for students to write *immediately* after the presentation of a stimulus like nonverbal movies, sensory awareness activities, or interpersonal encounters. Upon completion (not the next day), students read their papers aloud. (After the oral sharing, the papers are not read by anyone else unless students have time to revise and proofread.) Through comments and questions, teachers focus on the *differences* in the responses to the same stimulus.

As students share and focus on unique qualities of each paper, they begin to appreciate differences in approach, content, organization, flavor, and wording. Then students come to expect differences, and this expectation frees students to say or write their "own things" in their own ways.

The climate for sharing comes when appreciation and expectation of differences are well established. Then small groups, instead of the large group, may be used for oral sharing of impromptu writing, and peer evaluation may begin with revisions of work that has been orally shared.

To give direction to peer evaluation, teachers distribute the following questions to the small groups:

1 Identify the best section of the composition and describe what makes it effective.
2 Identify a sentence, a group of sentences, or a paragraph that needs revision, and revise it as a group, writing the final version on the back of the paper.
3 Identify one (or two) things the writer can do to improve his or her next piece of writing. Write these goals on the first page at the top.
4 (After the first evaluation, the following question should come first.) What were the goals the writer was working on? Were they reached? If not, identify those passages that need improvement and as a group revise those sections, writing final versions on the back of the paper. If revisions are necessary, set up the same goals for the next paper and delete question 3.

As with the questions for self-evaluation, teachers have found it helpful to vary them by deleting one of the questions and adding others related to aspects of composition dealt with in class.

As a class begins to engage in peer evaluation, various rating scales can provide useful structure. (See the Cooper and Lloyd-Jones chapters.) Teachers often begin peer evaluation by working through a rating scale with the entire class and sample papers. When students have the knack of using a scale, they break into small groups to have a go at it.

Students in high school have effectively used the rating procedures for expository writing developed by Diederich (1974). Sager (1973) found that sixth-grade students could use the rating scale she developed to evaluate and improve their writing. Although not dealing with rating scales, Lagana's research (1972) concluded that after specific goals for writing improvement had been established, peer evaluation was as effective as traditional teacher evaluation over a fifteen-week period.

Combining individualized learning activities and peer evaluation of compositions, Lagana's study centered on the development of a model for working with expository writing. For each composition assigned, each peer group selected its own topic and decided upon a writing objective from teacher-prepared lists. Individualized learning activities for each objective were available for students who wanted to work with them. At the end of the semester, the writing of the experimental group of thirty tenth-grade students (who had written ten compositions) and the writing of the control group (who had written six compositions) were compared. The results: peer evaluation was as effective as teacher evaluation; peer evaluation reduced the teacher's onerous burden of correcting papers after school and enabled students to write more frequently; individualized activities helped students progress at their own rate; peer groups provided more immediate feedback than did the teacher.

The results of these studies suggest that a progression may be established for peer evaluation. First, peer evaluation may center on the rating scales developed through various research projects. Next, students begin to assume more control by having peer groups select their own topics and goals for writing improvement from prepared lists. Finally, students may have enough experience and sophistication to use only the questions suggested in this chapter. Such a progression goes from highly structured experiences to less structured ones.

Rationale

Peer evaluation offers each student an opportunity to observe how his or her writing affects others. Because the most significant others in a teenager's life are peers, peer evaluation provides a kind of motivation not available in the other approaches to evaluation I have described. As trust and support grow in these small groups, students begin writing for peers, developing a sense of audience, becoming aware of their own voices, and using their voices to produce certain effects in others. This cognizance of audience and voice may develop early: when my older son was in third through fifth grades, he regularly "wrote books" and shared them with the same group of peers. He knew John would respond best to his science fiction stories, that Peter would appreciate his books of jokes and riddles, and that Karl would like his plays on words and experimentation.

Research studies dealing with peer groups and evaluation of writing (Lagana 1972; Maize 1952; Sutton and Allen 1964; Ford 1973; Pierson 1967; and Sager 1973) indicate that improvement in theme-writing ability and grammar usage, when small groups of students engage in peer evaluation, may equal or even exceed the improvement that occurs under evaluation procedures carried out by the teacher. Lagana, in particular, discovered that his experimental group improved more than the control group in organization, critical thinking, and sentence revision; the control group showed greater improvement in conventions. Ford found that the college freshmen in the experimental group showed significantly higher gains in both grammar and composition ability.

In addition, peer evaluation helps students to check their perceptions of reality and to correct distortions. For instance, last year some inner-city children working in a peer evaluation group were writing about snakes, and as they compared their descriptions of snakes, they found that one boy's snake had three eyes, another boy's had four legs, and a girl's slept in the summer and went ice-skating in the winter. After much merry discussion on their part, I sent them to the library to do some reading, and the librarian reported that they helped each other check out their perceptions, accommodating them to reality. On a more sophisticated level, students who believe that a particular passage conveys precisely what they mean often have to face the reality that none of their peers can understand the garbled expression.

Peer evaluation also strengthens the interpersonal skills needed for collaboration and cooperation as students identify strong and weak passages and revise ineffective ones, as they set goals for each other, and as they encourage risk-taking behaviors in writing. These evaluation procedures accommodate the needs McClelland et al. (1953) have identified in their work on achievement motivation. After basic needs are met, needs for affiliation, power, and achievement must be satisfied to produce growth. Seemingly, achievement is dependent upon fulfillment of the needs for affiliation and power. In their work with urban education, Weinstein and Fantini (1970) have identified three similar concerns: (1) "Concern about *self-image*"; (2) "Concern about *disconnectedness*, a wish to establish a connection with others or with society, at large, to know where one fits in the scheme of things"; (3) "Concern about *control* over one's life." Small peer groups help students develop a sense of self and relationship to others: "Who am I?" and "How do I fit in?" are the questions raised as a person works through affiliation needs in a small group and is accepted as an integral part of the group. When peers have regular opportunities to share their writing and to take part in evaluation procedures, they exercise power or control over decisions that affect their own work. Furthermore, as the dynamics of small-group work evolve, peers develop a sense of group inclusion, acceptance, support, trust, reality-testing, and collaboration.

Advantages and Disadvantages

The educational value of group work, the personal-growth potential, and the development of interpersonal skills make peer evaluation highly desirable for classroom use. Students seem to learn how to handle written language more effectively as they read what peers have written; peer models seem to be more efficacious than models from established writers. As peers collaborate to revise passages, they engage in taxing work, motivating them to diagnose what is wrong, prescribe what is needed, and then collectively struggle through revision procedures. Editing and revising become more palatable as group efforts, and when everyone in the group is stuck, the "teachable moment" comes forth.

Another advantage is that the teacher is relieved of spending countless hours on grading papers. Interestingly, all of the research studies on peer evaluation emphasize this point (Lagana 1972; Maize 1952; Sutton and Allen 1964; Ford 1973; Pierson 1967; and Sager 1973). Through the use of peer evaluation procedures, students are able to write more frequently and to receive more immediate feedback, and teachers have more time for individualized instruction and for conferences with students.

Yet there are disadvantages to peer evaluation. Group processes take time; groups that function well tend to spend half their time on process and half on task. If a curriculum has vast amounts of material to cover and if teachers feel compelled to cover everything, frustration is bound to set in unless teachers and students want to spend time on group processes. Interpersonal skills take time to develop, and many teachers may need the security of an inservice course or a summer school course in group work before they will feel sufficiently competent to use group procedures. (However, at times a school counselor with group skills has worked with a class and teacher until interpersonal skills were strengthened.)

Another problem that has emerged is that some teachers do not trust group processes. In one school, teachers working with peer evaluation were first reading the papers, tallying the mistakes, and developing class exercises to deal with the errors. After the group work, teachers read the evaluations and papers (again!), discovering that some peers were correcting passages with no mistakes. So teachers were correcting the miscorrections, spending an inordinate amount of time and becoming frustrated. Because peers obviously lack the sophistication of the teacher, they will misperceive some passages, but these distortions can be looked at diagnostically, since they illuminate where the students are and what *they* think is good and bad, effective and ineffective, correct and incorrect. Students' misperceptions can help the teacher determine where to begin instruction. Moreover, a teacher must allow students to have freedom to make mistakes and to develop confidence in their own perceptions and decisions. If a teacher is able to facilitate such group work, then peer evaluation has untapped potential for the improvement of student writing. It should be used much more extensively.

Summary

Individualized goal setting, self-evaluation, and peer evaluation have much to contribute to formative evaluation of writing in the classroom because the individual students become increasingly responsible for the direction and evaluation of their own growth in writing. Used initially, individualized goal setting develops a climate of trust and acceptance as a teacher gets to know students and their writing strengths and weaknesses. Later in the year, individualized goal setting helps students to see beyond their own horizons and gain a broader perspective of the possibilities in writing. Self-evaluation strengthens students' editing abilities, giving them control over decisions that affect their own writing growth as they learn to trust their own criteria of good writing. Peer evaluation helps student writers find their voices, develop a sense of audience, and experiment with revision strategies.

After introducing the three evaluation procedures, teachers may want to divide the year into blocks of two, three, or four weeks during which one-third of a class works closely with the teacher on individualized goal setting, another third uses self-evaluation strategies, and the last third engages in peer evaluation. When the time is up, students change to another kind of discourse and another approach to evaluation.

While the above is going on, teachers may want to introduce a variety of ways of describing/responding/evaluating and have students experiment with these as they compose, revise, and evaluate their own writing. This book should provide some ideas that can be adapted for students to use as they engage in peer and self-evaluation. In an ideal situation, students should have an acquaintance with a large repertoire of evaluation techniques and approaches and should be able to decide which one of these would prove most helpful for each paper in its various stages.

Bibliography

Allott, M., ed. *Novelists on the Novel*. New York: Columbia University Press, 1959.

Alschuler, A. *Developing Achievement Motivation in Adolescents: Education for Human Growth*. Englewood Cliffs, N. J.: Educational Technology Publications, 1973.

Alschuler, A.; Tabor, D.; and McIntyre, J. *Teaching Achievement Motivation: Theory and Practice in Psychological Education*. Middletown, Conn.: Education Ventures, 1970.

Arnold, L. V. "Writer's Cramp and Eyestrain—Are They Paying Off?" *English Journal* 53 (1964):10-15.

Axline, V. *Dibs: In Search of Self*. Boston: Houghton Mifflin, 1964.

Bata, E.J. "A Study of the Relative Effectiveness of Marking Techniques on Junior College Freshman English Composition." Ph.D. dissertation, University of Maryland, 1972. *Dissertation Abstracts International* (1973):73-17028.

Beach, R. "Self-Evaluation Strategies of Extensive Revisers and Nonrevisers." *College Composition and Communication* 27 (1976):160-64.

Braddock, R.; Lloyd-Jones, R.; and Schoer, L. *Research in Written Composition*. Urbana, Ill.: National Council of Teachers of English, 1963.

Buxton, E. W. "An Experiment to Test the Effects of Writing Frequency and Guided Practice upon Students' Skill in Written Expression." Ph.D. dissertation, Stanford University, 1958.

Cazden, C. B. *Child Language and Education*. New York: Holt, Rinehart and Winston, 1972.

Coleman, V. B. "A Comparison between the Relative Effectiveness of Marginal, Interlinear, and Terminal Commentary and of Audiotaped Commentary in Responding to English Compositions." Ph.D. dissertation, University of Pittsburgh, 1972. *Dissertation Abstracts International* (1973):73-04121.

Cooper, C. "Measuring Growth in Writing." "Research Roundup," *English Journal* 64 (March 1975):111-20.

deCharms, R. *Personal Causation: The Internal Affective Determinants of Behavior*. New York: Academic Press, 1968.

Diederich, P. *Measuring Growth in English*. Urbana, Ill.: National Council of Teachers of English, 1974.

Ekstein, R., and Motto, R. L., comp. *From Learning for Love to Love of Learning: Essays on Psychoanalysis and Education*. New York: Brunner/Mazel, 1969.

Ford, B. W. "The Effects of Peer Editing/Grading on the Grammar-Usage and Theme-Composition Ability of College Freshmen." Ed. D. dissertation, University of Oklahoma, 1973. *Dissertation Abstracts International* (1973):73-15321.

Fromm, E. *Man for Himself: An Inquiry into the Psychology of Ethics*. New York: Holt, Rinehart and Winston, 1947.

_____. *Escape from Freedom*. New York: Avon Books, 1966.

Groff, P. "Does Negative Criticism Discourage Children's Compositions?" *Elementary English* 52 (1975):1032-34.

Haggitt, T. W. *Working with Language*. Oxford, England: Blackwell, 1969.

Jerabek, R., and Dieterich, D. "Composition Evaluation: The State of the Art." *College Composition and Communication* 26 (1975):183-86.

Jourard, S. M. *Personal Adjustment: An Approach through the Study of Healthy Personality.* 2d ed. New York: Macmillan, 1963.

Lagana, J. R. "The Development, Implementation, and Evaluation of a Model for Teaching Composition Which Utilizes Individualized Learning and Peer Grouping." Ph.D. dissertation, University of Pittsburgh, 1972. *Dissertation Abstracts International* (1973):73-04127.

Macrorie, K. *Uptaught.* New York: Hayden Book Co., 1970.

Maize, R. C. "A Study of Two Methods of Teaching English Composition to Retarded College Freshmen." Ph.D. dissertation, Purdue University, 1952.

Maslow, A. *Toward a Psychology of Being.* Princeton, N. J.: Van Nostrand Co., 1962.

———. *The Farther Reaches of Human Nature.* New York: Viking Press, 1971.

McClelland, D. C.; Atkinson, J. W.; Clark, R. A.; and Lowell, E. L. *The Achievement Motive.* New York: Appleton-Century-Crofts, 1953.

Miller, H. *On Writing.* Edited by Thomas Moore. New York: A New Directions Book, 1964.

Nin, A. *The Novel of the Future.* New York: Macmillan, 1968.

Otto, H. A. *Group Methods Designed to Actualize Human Potential: A Handbook.* Chicago: Achievement Motivation Systems, 1968.

Pierson, H. "Peer and Teacher Correction: A Comparison of the Effects of Two Methods of Teaching Composition in Grade Nine English Classes." Ph.D. dissertation, New York University, 1967.

Raths, L. E.; Harmin, M.; and Simon, S. B. *Values and Teaching.* Columbus, Ohio: Charles Merrill, 1966.

Rogers, C. *On Becoming a Person.* Boston: Houghton Mifflin, 1961.

———. "Toward a Theory of Creativity." *A Sourcebook for Creative Thinking.* Edited by S. J. Purnes and H. F. Harding. New York: Charles Scribner's Sons, 1962.

Rogers, C., and Dymond, R. F., ed. *Psychotherapy and Personality Change: Coordinated Research Studies in the Client-Centered Approach.* Chicago: University of Chicago Press, 1954.

Sager, C. *Improving the Quality of Written Composition through Pupil Use of Rating Scale.* Ann Arbor, Mich.: University Microfilms, 1973. Order no. 73-23 605.

Sax, S., and Hollander, S. *Reality Games.* New York: Macmillan, 1972.

Schroeder, T. S. "The Effects of Positive and Corrective Written Teacher Feedback on Selected Writing Behaviors of Fourth-Grade Children." Ph.D. dissertation, University of Kansas, 1973. *Dissertation Abstracts International* (1973):73-30869.

Smith, F. M. *Comprehension and Learning.* New York: Holt, Rinehart and Winston, 1975.

Stanford, G., and Stanford, B. D. *Learning Discussion Skills through Games.* New York: Citation Press, 1969.

Stanton, B. E. "A Comparison of Theme Grades Written by Students Possessing Varying Amounts of Cumulative Written Guidance: Checklist, Instruction, and Questions and Feedback." Ed.D. dissertation, Brigham Young University, 1973. *Dissertation Abstracts International* (1974):74-23646.

Stevens, A. E. "The Effects of Positive and Negative Evaluation on the Written Composition of Low Performing High School Students." Ed.D. dissertation, Boston University, 1973. *Dissertation Abstracts International* (1973):73-23617.

Sutton, J. T., and Allen, E. D. "The Effect of Practice and Evaluation on Improve-
    ment in Written Composition." Cooperative Research Project, no. 1993. De
    Land, Fla.: Stetson University, 1964.
Underwood, D. J. "Evaluating Themes: Five Studies and an Application of One
    Study." M.A. thesis, University of Illinois, 1968.
Weinstein, G., and Fantini, M., ed. *Toward Humanistic Education: A Curriculum
    of Affect.* New York: Praeger Publishers, 1970.
Wormsbecker, J. H. "A Comparative Study of Three Methods of Grading Com-
    positions." M.A. thesis, University of British Columbia, 1955.
Yalom, I. D. *The Theory and Practice of Group Psychotherapy.* 2d ed. New York:
    Basic Books, 1975.